IS THIS TRUE?
—— OR ——
ARE YOU BEING A WISE GUY?

THIRD EDITION

BRUCE R. KINDIG

Copyright © 2022 Bruce R. Kindig.

All rights reserved. No part of this book may be reproduced, stored, or transmitted by any means—whether auditory, graphic, mechanical, or electronic—without written permission of both publisher and author, except in the case of brief excerpts used in critical articles and reviews. Unauthorized reproduction of any part of this work is illegal and is punishable by law.

ISBN: 979-8-88640-145-5 (sc)
ISBN: 979-8-88640-146-2 (hc)
ISBN: 979-8-88640-147-9 (e)

Because of the dynamic nature of the Internet, any web addresses or links contained in this book may have changed since publication and may no longer be valid. The views expressed in this work are solely those of the author and do not necessarily reflect the views of the publisher, and the publisher hereby disclaims any responsibility for them.

One Galleria Blvd., Suite 1900, Metairie, LA 70001
1-888-421-2397

CONTENTS

Introduction v

Chapter 1   Easy Questions to Get Started 1

Chapter 2   Funny Stuff 8

Chapter 3   Puzzles for Wise Guys 20

Chapter 4   The Meanings of Yogi-isms 40

Chapter 5   The Heart of the Issue 49

Chapter 6   Answers to Covid-19 Questions 80

Chapter 7   Answers to Stupid Questions 87

About the Author 139

Other Books written by Bruce R. Kindig 140

INTRODUCTION

What is truth? This book may or may not answer that for you. Truth is like beauty; it is in the eyes of the beholder. It is not the purpose of this book to tell lies, so you will just read about different ways to tell the truth. In life, we often come across tidbits of useful, or sometimes useless, information. This book will have some of both.

Several years ago, I wrote the book *Words of Wisdom from Anonymous Wiseguys* under the pen name of John Marsh. It was a book about wisdom. It was also about stupidity. Using a question and answer format the book examined stupid questions; if there really is such a thing. Answers were given to the questions that were sometimes serious and at other times a wise guy would make a crack about the stupid question and literally give a stupid answer. Oh, what fun it is to make fun of other people and how they think about things.

This book is not intended to be politically correct. In fact, we may make fun of the political correct assumed answers. Names in this book are generic assumptions of perhaps, someone you know. Sometimes we will use the name of some soldier who may be doing something under the supervision of a sergeant or corporal. The smartest person is going to be Captain Scott. Although the good captain was a real officer in the American Civil War, he wasn't anything like what you will read in this book.

If you are offended by anything in this book, then you should put it down and burn it in your microwave oven. This book is not about you, but if you resemble anyone in this book, well then, congratulations.

Are you a wise guy? Then you may join the ranks of those who enjoy the answers. This book will follow the format of questions and answers most of the time. One of the chapters will be word puzzles to try to stump the wise guys. Good luck with that one.

The Yogi chapter in this book is about real people. It is all in good fun, even Yogi thought so. The Covid-19 chapter is so much fun to see how our government really helped us out of a pandemic. Who would have thought we would all follow these rules like cattle heading for the slaughter house.

This book contains the truth about common sense. The wise guys use satire, cynicism and sometimes double talk to help bring you to know the truth.

CHAPTER 1

EASY QUESTIONS TO GET STARTED

Q. What is the hardest thing to learn in college?
A. How to open a beer bottle with a quarter.

Q. What are the sins of omission?
A. They are the sins we should have committed.

Q. If the sergeant asked for all morons to step forward what should I do?
A. Step forward so the sergeant won't be standing there alone.

Q. Will the encyclopedia tell you everything you will ever need to know?
A. Not if you're married.

Q. What is a bigamist?
A. A man who makes the same mistake twice at the same time.

Q. What should you do when you and your wife have a difference of opinion?
A. Don't tell her yours.

Q. I want to say something soft and sweet to my sweet heart. Do you have any suggestions?
A. Try custard pie and see how that goes.

Q. I've heard that a marriage license is the most expensive license there is. Is that true?
A. Yes, it costs $10 at the courthouse and the rest of your income for life.

Q. Can you name two convictions that carry a life sentence?
A. Murder and marriage.

Q. I noticed that my car insurance policy would not pay cash for an accident but just give me a replacement vehicle. Is this a good policy?
A. It's okay for your car but you might want to check the fine print on the life insurance policy you have on your wife.

Q. I've noticed that the tonic I bought from the salesman for my bad cough says that it works so well that I will never use any other. Do you think this is true?
A. Sure, but you might want to try something less fatal.

Q. Women always accuse a man when the toilet seat is left up. I don't think that is fair.
A. Neither does HQ staff. If a woman won't look at the toilet before using it, what else will she back her ass up to without looking?

Q. Is there any benefit to being grossly over-weight?
A. Yes, you will be less likely to be kidnapped.

Q. What is a reenactor?
A. Not to be confused with identity theft, he is pretending to be someone else.

Q. What is something you would like to give but not receive?
A. Advise.

Q. What is the proper amount of time to be engaged before getting married?
A. If it is more than six months the girl is still seeing if she can do better than you.

Q. What does a man gain by making numerous mistakes?
A. He gains experience. The rest of us gain funny stories.

Q. What do you call an optimist who practices what he preaches?
A. A pessimist.

Q. Do politicians seem like they are going somewhere?
A. Sure. First, they run for office and then they run for cover.

Q. Is a philanthropist a stamp collector?
A. Oh you simple-minded fool. No, he is someone who returns to the people publicly a small percentage of his wealth that he steels from them privately.

Q. What makes a person popular?
A. The ability to know a whole lot of uninteresting people.

Q. When will I hear people praise me for the things I have done?
A. You will have to wait for your funeral.

Q. What makes a person a radical?
A. They have a different opinion than you.

Q. What is a self-made man?
A. It's a horrible example of unskilled labor.

Q. Can you think of a reason why I shouldn't tip?

A. Why should you pay the wages of someone else's worker?

Q. Where can I find a person who thinks the world can't go on without him?
A. The cemetery is full of them.

Q. What is the best advise that I can give?
A. None. Keep your mouth shut if you know what's good for you.

Q. When company comes and stays at my house they tend to stay longer than I expected. How do I get them to leave without being rude?
A. Start treating them like family.

Q. How can an author increase his book sales?
A. Have the book banned at the local library, then sell copies out of the trunk of your car.

Q. What do you call a person who tries to teach stupid people?
A. A jackass whisperer.

Q. Why do dogs retrieve a ball when you throw it?
A. Dogs think you like to throw balls and it amuses them.

Q. Is poison ever safe to consume?
A. Yes, it is no longer poisonous after the expiration date. But more important- why do you want to know this?

Q. Which letter is silent in the word "scent," the S or the C?
A. The S is silent. It is always the first letter when 2 consonants are together at the beginning of a word. Example: pneumonia and psycho and philharmonic. The P is silent in every case.

Q. Do twins ever not like their twin?
A. Rarely, usually after finding out that one of them was not planned.

Q. Why is the letter W, in English, called a double U? Shouldn't it be a double V?
A. It's a double U because it is a vowel.

Q. Is oxygen considered to be a dangerous gas?
A. It should be, but it often takes 75 to 100 years to kill you.

Q. Is cleaning your house a waste of time?
A. Yes, because you are just moving the dirt around and that makes something else dirty.

Q. Can someone intentionally lose a game of rock, paper, scissors?
A. The answer is no, but I am sure you can.

Q. Can someone predict the future?
A. Your future self is watching you right now through memories.

Q. Doctors in 1953 predicted that Stephan Hawking had only two years to live. What ever happened to them?
A. They all died before he did. There is a lesson here. Do you see it?

Q. What is the answer to the question What, Where and When?
A. Replace the W with a T for each word. Now you have the answer.

Q. Do animals need glasses?
A. Many animals probably do need glasses. Why don't you go catch a possum and give him an eye test?

Q. How can I reduce the number of holes in a net?

A. Staff is not sure why you want to do this, but we can tell you this: rip a hole in a net and you will now have fewer holes in the net than you had before.

Q. Am I weird for living in my own world?
A. Not really. At least everyone knows you there.

Q. If flying is so safe, why do they call the airport the terminal?
A. Because that is where the bodies are taken after a crash.

Q. Are there really two sides to every divorce?
A. Yes, yours and the jerks.

Q. Do you know what record I broke today?
A. Your previous record for the number of days you've stayed alive.

Q. Why can't we have a smoking section in every restaurant?
A. For the same reason that every swimming pool does not have a peeing section.

Q. What is the hardest word to master in the English language?
A. The word is ass.

Q. Could you explain why ass is the hardest word to understand?
A. I suppose you think ass means butt. That could be true but it has so many more meanings. For instance, what is a lazy ass? If you say "my lazy ass husband" is he actually lazy without the word ass? The word ass has absolutely no meaning in this way. So, what is a long ass flight? A long flight, as there is not butt in the meaning of the word. You can actually add the word ass to any sentence for absolutely no change to the meaning of the sentence except that it sounds cool. Using the word ass can also change the meaning of a

word. For instance, a badass is actually good even though bad is bad but a dumb-ass is still dumb. If someone tells you to move your ass, now they are talking about your entire person not your butt. But if someone said they had a fast ass car, and you said, "fast my ass", you are saying no to the car being fast. Now if you divide ass such as half ass; that means something is done badly and a piece of ass is good to have.

Q. Is there anything else about the word ass?
A. You're either covering it, laughing it off, kicking it, busting it, kissing it, trying to get a piece of it, behaving like one or you live with one.

CHAPTER 2

FUNNY STUFF

Q. Do men and women see the same things?
A. No, men can't see wrinkles in clothes.

Q. Is it true that food makes a good substitute for sex?
A. Yes, but those who have tried it now can't even get into their own pants.

Q. What pills should never be taken together?
A. Off hand, laxatives and sleeping pills come to mind.

Q. My wife said I am like a fine wine. What did she mean?
A. Men start out like grapes and it's up to women to stomp the crap out of them until they turn into something acceptable to have with dinner.

Q. I am a little clumsy with a knife when I slice vegetables. What should I do?
A. Get someone else to hold them while you chop away.

Q. What should I do about a bad cough?
A. Take a large dose of laxatives, then you will be afraid to cough.

Q. My wife argues with me about leaving the toilet seat up. What can I do?
A. Avoid arguments by leaving the seat down and start peeing in the sink.

Q. Should I eat more natural foods?
A. You can take your chances but most people die of natural causes.

Q. Why will a man pay $2 for a $1 Item?
A. Because he needs the item, whereas a woman will pay $1 for a $2 item that she doesn't need.

Q. I'm having a party on Friday. What should I use for a centerpiece at the table?
A. Anything; as long as it was not prepared by a taxidermist.

Q. What should I do to keep potatoes from budding?
A. Buy Hungry Jack mashed potato mix, keep it in the pantry for up to a year. Keep it dry and you can go two years.

Q. Should I brush some beaten egg whites over piecrust before baking to yield a glossy finish?
A. Don't do it. Brushing egg whites is not on the directions of Mrs. Smith frozen pie.

Q. Is it true that you can cure a headache by rubbing a lime on your forehead?
A. You are getting bad advice. Mix the lime with tequila, chill and drink.

Q. What should I do with leftover wine?
A. We don't know. We have never heard of that.

Q. If you are going to make a parachute jump, at least how high should you be?
A. Three days of steady drinking should do it.

Q. Which of your five senses diminishes, as you get older?
A. Sense of decency.

Q. If you teach a child how to be polite and courteous are there any problems they can't handle when they become adults?
A. Yes, how to merge onto the freeway.

Q. I only have $12.15 to my name. How will I be able to live in retirement?
A. You have all the money you will ever need if you die by 4:30.

Q. What is a whack?
A. It is when something doesn't work right, like it is out of whack.

Q. I have dyslexia, can you help me to read?
A. Yes, just cross your eyes when you read.

Q. How many men does it take to open a beer?
A. None, it should already be opened when she brings it.

Q. Why is a Laundromat a bad place to pick up women?
A. Because, a woman who can't afford a washing machine probably can't support you.

Q. How do you fix a woman's watch?
A. You don't. There is a clock on the stove.

Q. If your dog is barking at the back door and your wife is yelling at the front door, who do you let in first?
A. The dog. He will shut up as soon as you let him in.

Q. What food will diminish a woman's sex drive by 90%.
A. Wedding cake.

Q. Do they sell perfume in South Carolina?
A. No, you will have to bring your own. People there don't stink.

Q. When the end of the world comes, where is the best place to be?
A. Arkansas, because everything happens in Arkansas about 20 years later than everywhere else in the world.

Q. Why is air like sex?
A. Because it's no big deal unless you're not getting any.

Q. Should I be afraid of getting wrinkles?
A. No, because they don't hurt.

Q. Could you describe friendship in a way that I can understand?
A. Friendship is like peeing your pants, everyone can see it, but only you can feel the true warmth.

Q. What's the difference between a northern fairy tale and a southern fairy tale?
A. A northern fairy tale starts off with "Once upon a time...." And a southern fairy tale begins with "Y'all ain't gonna believe this shit......."

Q. What is the hereafter?
A. It is your final destination, as in entering a room and saying "wonder what I'm here after."

Q. If 4 out of 5 people suffer from diarrhea, does that mean that one out of five enjoys it?
A. Absolutely, he's the one that made it to the toilet and laughs at the rest of you who didn't.

Q. How hard is it to get a 4.0 in college?
A. Not too hard. Many students achieve a 4.0 every Saturday night.

Q. How long is a minute?
A. It depends on which side of the door you are on.

Q. What is the oldest recorded writing about PMS?
A. It is found in Mathew 14 verse 94. "And Mary rode Joseph's ass all the way to Egypt."

Q. How could we discourage inbreeding?
A. Ban country music.

Q. What do you see when you watch the people at Wal-Mart?
A. That God has a sense of humor.

Q. What is the best way to handle stress?
A. Do what a dog would do. If you can't eat it or hump it, then piss on it and walk away.

Q. What's a good thing about a bad decision?
A. They make good stories.

Q. What should never be said while sitting on the toilet in a public rest room?
A. Uh oh, I knew I shouldn't put my lips on that.

Q. Is it true that I lose brain cells every time I get drunk?
A. Yes, but it appears that you replace them with fat cells.

Q. Can you name six animals that live specifically in the Arctic?
A. How about two polar bears and four seals.

Q. Do you think I should see a psychic?
A. Don't waste your money. Wait until you see the newspaper headline that reads: "Psychic Wins Lottery."

Q. Why is my wife so beautiful but so stupid?
A. God made her beautiful so you would be attracted to her. He also made her stupid so she would be attracted to you.

Q. What is the best way to die?
A. Like your grandmother, in her sleep. Not yelling and screaming like everyone else in her car.

Q. If my wife sits down next to me when I am flipping the channels and she asks, "What's on TV?" What should I tell her?
A. Anything, but don't say dust.

Q. My wife's birthday is next month and she hinted that she wants something shiny that goes from 0 to 150 in about 3 seconds. What should I get her?
A. A scale.

Q. What was the Pope's first miracle?
A. He made a lame man blind.

Q. Why does my dog bite people?
A. He doesn't like them.

Q. In what state was Abraham Lincoln born?
A. Naked and screaming just like everyone else.

Q. Restaurant rules - No Shirt, No Shoes, No Service. What if someone goes in with No Pants? Would the restaurant serve them?
A. According to the rules, yes. But the chair you sat in will have to be burned.

Q. Are eyebrows considered facial hair?
A. If they are on your face the answer is yes. If they are on your ass consider them pubic hair.

Q. If a woman wears thong underwear, will she whistle when she farts?
A. Yes, if she could whistle before she wore the thong.

Q. I overheard that Captain Scott said my brain was like the Bermuda Triangle. What does that mean?
A. All knowledge that goes into it is never found again.

Q. Can a cemetery raise its prices and blame it on the cost of living?
A. No it is the cost of dying that is going up. Just think how much money you can save by dying today. Hint.

Q. A soldier was overheard talking about Captain Scott in such a way that he said that there is no difference between him and the captain. Can you name just one difference between this soldier and Captain Scott?
A. Captain Scott does not scream when he pees.

Q. Do you yawn in your sleep?
A. Of course. Do a self-test. Sit up all night and see if you yawn.

Q. If someone with their nose pierced has a cold, and they take their nose ring out, does snot come out of the piercing hole when they sneeze?
A. Yes. There is a lot of pressure from a sneeze. Just don't pierce your butt cheek, could be messy.

Q. If there's a speed of sound and a speed of light, is there a speed of smell?
A. Yes. Smell travels at the speed of wind. Check out the speed of the men moving away from the campfire when someone breaks wind. Use a stopwatch to measure the time it takes to hear the rumble to the point where the men begin to move.

Q. If I can hear my own heartbeat, do I need to be concerned?
A. If you don't hear your own heartbeat you need to be concerned.

Q. If a fart smells bad, am I sick?
A. You better believe it. Do you really think smelling very bad is normal?

Q. Should I light a match to get rid of the fart smell?
A. Yes, you are the one to do that.

Q. Can you plan a surprise birthday party for a psychic?
A. Yes, but he will know that it's his party. To fool a psychic Captain Scott suggests that you hold a party for someone else and not on the psychic's birthday. Then tell the psychic happy birthday. When he says it is not his birthday just show him the calendar with today's date circled with his name in it. Then tell him, "If you're a psychic why didn't you tell me last week that it wasn't your birthday today when I marked the calendar?"

Q. What would happen to the sea's water level if every boat in the world is taken out of the water at the same time?

A. Simple physics would say that the water level would go down by the amount of water displaced by the removed boats. When your 275-pound body goes into a bathtub the water rises and when you get out, the water lowers back to the original level plus what you just peed in the water. The unknown factor is the amount of pee in the water which would be the flow of rivers into the seas. Another factor would be all of the sunken items in the seas represented by the "Baby Ruth" you left in the tub. (Baby Ruth? What?) Go rent Caddy Shack.

Q. Do all-boys schools have a girl's bathroom?

A. The answer is no. However, recently students can choose their own gender. A boy can now say he's a girl without showing he's nuts. (Or is that his nuts?) Rumor has it that the sergeant is a lesbian. Go figure.

Q. Do the English people eat English muffins, or are they just called muffins?

A. Yes, they eat English muffins no matter what you want to call them. Do the French eat French fries? Of course, even though they don't call them that. The English can call their food anything they want just like you do. All of the men ate donkey stew even though there was no donkey in it. But watch out for shit on a shingle because it just might be that.

Q. Why are dog's noses always wet?

A. Because they are unable to wipe their noses on their sleeves like you. Captain Scott suggests that you improve the well-being of dogs by wiping their noses for them. You should start with General Bragg's pit bull.

Q. Why don't women put pictures of their missing husbands on beer cans?
A. They would if they wanted him back.

Q. If a deaf person has to go to court, is it still called a hearing?
A. Yes, it is and that is why they stick that big horn in the deaf person's ear. If you are going to play the deaf card, we're going to play the "look stupid" card.

Q. If a clown farts, does it smell funny? (Various answers)
A. Aren't all farts funny? You don't have to be a clown to fart. Just look around the campfire.
A. I'm afraid of clowns, so if one farts I am afraid he will explode all over me.
A. It's only funny if it sounds juicy. Who wouldn't laugh at a clown with shitty pants.
A. If it is humor you want, Captain Scott suggests you all wear clown costumes around the campfire.

Q. What is the secret of life?
A. Everyone knows that there are four elements that make life possible. Captain Scott has watched the men during fatigue call and has a theory that not all men are given an equal amount of each element. Some men have more of the bad element and some have less. The elements are protons, neutrons, electrons and morons.

Q. If a bee is allergic to pollen would it get the hives?
A. Yes. If you were allergic to knowledge, would you be a moron?

Q. Will trying to stifle a fart make it louder?
A. Yes, and good luck with that.

Q. Can you cry under water?
A. Let's run a test. You go under water and someone will drop a brick on your head. When you come up let's see if you are crying.

Q. What do you call male ballerinas?
A. Sissies

Q. Why do they say "easy as pie"? Making a pie is not that easy.
A. True. But eating pie sure is easy.

Q. Do married people really live longer than single people?
A. No, it just seems longer

Q. Why aren't lawyers sworn in during trials?
A. Then they wouldn't be able to lie.

Q. Is it true that Captain Scott was once a world-class athlete? I heard that he was able to jump higher than a two-story building in Memphis. Is that true?
A. Yes, because buildings in Memphis can't jump.

Q. What is the difference between ignorance and innocence?
A. If you're 2 years old and you overturn your plate of spaghetti onto your head at a fine restaurant, its innocence. If you're 32 years old, it's ignorance. The reverse is the case for the person who took you there each time.

Q. Why is it that our high school experiences occupy such a prominent place in our memories?
A. During high school we develop the most vigorous bodies we will ever have. At the same time, we possess the least amount of sense we will ever have. This combination produces many memorable moments.

Q. What is a garbanzo bean?
A. The stuff on the bottom of your plate that you say looks like shit.

Q. Is it legal to name your kid "Anonymous"?
A. Of course. Several people have that name and I'll bet you don't know a single one of them.

Q. If you dig a hole in the South Pole are you digging up or down?
A. If the dirt begins to fall on top of you then you are digging up.

Q. How do you get off a nonstop flight?
A. The same way you got off the train to Louisville. Open the door and jump.

Q. What do you call a fart that sounds like someone stomped on a ketchup packet?
A. An overachiever; you better check your undies.

Q. When I put a sheet over my head for Halloween, am I a ghost?
A. No, you are a mattress, that's what sheets cover.

Q. Do illiterate people like alphabet soup?
A. Yes, but they don't get the full effect of the alphabet soup. Probably why you don't care for it that much since you think it is making fun of you.

CHAPTER 3

PUZZLES FOR WISE GUYS

OK wise guys- figure this out:

1. Everyone knows that New Year's Day traditionally follows Christmas Day by one week. For example, if Christmas is a Monday, then New Year's Day will be on a Monday one week later. So, what is the last year in which Christmas and New Year's Day fell on different days of the week?
2. Answer- This year. When you look at Christmas first, the two holidays are exactly a week apart, but in different years. If you look at the two holidays in the same year they are a little over 51 weeks apart and on different days.

Anyone old enough to know the answer to this one?

1. Quote: "The Ford dealer sold me the deluxe model for only a dollar more, and I often stop by the Ford dealership and get fuel for just five cents a pound." Unquote. What are we talking about here? You couldn't get this at a Chevrolet or Buick dealer. Don't even think about it at the Hyundai or Toyota dealer either.
2. Henry Ford was a cheapskate. To provide the wooden panels for his station wagons, he had his own lumberyard. He hated

to see scrap wasted so he had the leftovers made into charcoal briquettes. To create a market for them he forced Ford dealerships to sell backyard grills. It cost 2 dollars for the cheapo grill and 3 bucks for the deluxe model.

Let's see how lucky you are with this one.

1. You take your wife to the grocery store. She has purchased the following items: Filippo Olive Oil, a family size tube of Preparation H, chunky peanut butter, chlorine bleach, iceberg lettuce, a Butterfinger candy bar and cheez whiz. When you start the car, you realize that you are stuck on some ice. Which of the items is most likely to help?
2. Are you choosing something and hoping to get lucky? Captain Scott recently tested the chlorine bleach on Pvt. Fitzpatrick's Mini Cooper. After pouring the bleach over all of the tires the car moved off of the ice but got stuck on the pavement. The bleach softened the rubber of the tires and made it sticky. It also ruined the tires, so I think you made the wrong choice. Maybe you should have tried the peanut butter, but don't use the Butterfinger, that is your treat for waiting two hours in the car for your wife to buy all those groceries. And leave the Cheez Whiz alone, that's hers.

If you ever had a VW bug you should know what happened in this one:

1. Before Cpl. Sailhorst was in the army he had a VW Beetle. One day his car wouldn't run so here is what he did: He loosened three bolts, replaced something, and tightened the bolts. The car ran great for six weeks and then he took 4 of his buddies and decided to pick up some babes. Unfortunately, the car burst into flames. What had Sailhorst done?

2. Sailhorst replaced a battery which was located under the back seat, but he used the wrong battery- the terminals were too tall. When his buddy Lardbutt sat in back, the springs touched the battery and the seat caught on fire. A smoldering VW is not exactly a good babe magnet.

Do you know your wood?

1. Owen McGrath was recently in West Virginia and took a tour of a coal mine. He discovered that the timbers used in the mine were poplar. He wondered why they didn't use something stronger like oak or ash. He knew that poplar was best to use in a mine, do you?
2. When poplar begins to buckle from the weight above it, it cracks with a loud noise which provides a warning to those in the mine. Now you know why he got out of there in time to tell HQ. He didn't mention if his wife knew the answer. Hmmm?

Are you wise enough to solve this mystery?

1. It's a dark stormy might. A watchman is making his rounds in a warehouse. He turns a corner. On the other side of a closed door at the end of the hall he hears, "No Frank, don't shoot!" and then a bang. The watchman enters the room and there is a doctor, a lawyer and plumber standing over the dead body. The gun is on the floor. The watchman says to the plumber, "You are under arrest for murder." How does he know it is the plumber?
2. He knows it is the plumber because the doctor and lawyer are women, and neither is named Frank.

Only upper crust travelers know this term, do you?

1. When the British travelled to what was then called the colony of India they went by ship. If you had some pull you would ask for a cabin on the port, or left, side of the ship on the way to India. On the way home, you would ask for a starboard cabin. From this peculiar custom, a word was invented. What was that word? Clue: blimey, crumpet, knickers, cricket.
2. Did you fall for one of the clues? Of course, that was just to throw you off because the word is so obvious that only the wisest of you would get it. The word is posh. It stood for port out, starboard home. On the way to India, the hot afternoon sun is on the starboard side and on the way back it was on the port side. Travelers wanted the cooler side and not the sunny side.

More words of wisdom

1. If you ever changed spark plugs you know that you must keep any dirt from falling into the spark plug holes. You could use your shop-vac to suck out any dirt before putting in the new spark plugs. What would happen if you do that?
2. Captain Scott used Pvt. Long's 1986 Yugo to see what would happen. Pvt. Jackson smuggled the car keys out and then ran the shop-vac. The result was an immediate explosion caused by sucking some air and gasoline into the vacuum motor. Jackson is alright, just a little frazzled.

Just another trick question

1. A blind man enters the subway with his seeing eye dog. The dog takes him to a booth where the sign says "Tokens, 40 cents."

While the dog pees on the sign the man rummages through his pocket and hands the vendor a dollar. No words are spoken, no hand gestures, no notes, nothing. The vendor has never seen him before and it is doubtful that the blind man had have seen the vendor. The vendor hands him two tokens and 20 cents change. How did the vendor know he wanted two tokens and not one?

2. Obviously, he handed the vendor four quarters. If he only wanted one token he would have only given two quarters.

Here is another puzzle for the wise guys:

1. Three travelers stop at a motel and ask for the cheapest room. The clerk charges them $30 and gives them the key to the laundry room. Later the clerk feels guilty for over charging the travelers. So, he gives the bell hop $5 to give the three idiots in the laundry room. The bell hop knows they can't divide $5 three ways evenly so he keeps $2 and give the travelers $3. Each traveler paid $10 and got a dollar back. That's $9 each or a total of $27. The bell hop got $2. That's $29. Where is the other dollar? If you don't know this then you fail the wise guy test.
2. There is no missing dollar. The travelers paid $25 for the room, they got $3 back from the clerk and the bell hop got $2. That adds up to $30.

More wise guys

1. Here is a household task you might do every day. You ask for advice, "is 50 enough?" "How about 125? No, that's not enough either. Maybe you should try 90." What is the task? Clue, when isn't 125 more than 90?

2. When you punch in 9, 0- that is more than punching in 1, 2, 5 on the microwave.

This makes perfect sense. Let's see if you know this.

1. An American tourist was visiting in Europe when he decided to buy a motorcycle. The salesman asked if he was going to send it to America. He said yes. The salesman said that he would have to change something on the motorcycle when he gets to America but he does not have any to sell him in Europe. What will he have to change to make the motorcycle legal to drive in America?
2. He will have to change the headlight. He bought it in England where they drive on the left side of the road so the headlight points slightly to the left. When driving on the right side of the road it will blind oncoming traffic.

Take this you wise guys.

1. A man went to the store and went to a certain aisle and asked the salesperson, "How much does 1 cost?" The salesperson said, "One costs 99 cents." "OK, how about 12?" "oh, that will be 1 dollar and 98 cents." "OK, in that case I'll take 128." The cashier rang up the purchase and it came out to be 2 dollars and 97 cents. What is this person buying? Music sounds as you wise guys try to figure this out. Maybe we should have bought 5744 for $3.96 and brought up the battery wagon to haul it back to camp.
2. The person was buying house numbers and each one cost 99 cents. Duh!!

You old timers might know this

1. Years ago, tanker trucks carrying flammable liquids had large chains hanging from the undercarriage which went from the undercarriage to the ground. It often threw out sparks while the truck was moving. Why were they dragging these chains and why don't they do that anymore? (Hint- it has nothing to do with the chain crop.)
2. By dragging chains the truck was constantly discharging its static charge with a series of small sparks that were far enough away to prevent a fireball the size of, say Toledo. Today, trucks have a ground strap that they attach to the underground tank so when the nozzle goes into the tank we have by far singed fewer eyebrows than we used to.

Did you find a rare treasure?

1. Recently, Joe's grandfather died in Dearborn, Michigan and when he went through his belongings he discovered a letter written to Henry Ford and signed by President William McKinley. The letter said, "Dear Mr. Ford, thank you for your offer to present a gift of one two-cylinder, four-cycle gasoline engine-powered quadricycle that you have developed in your workshop in Detroit for the use of the president. I do not feel that can replace our carriages at the White House with your machine which may not have the proper safety and comfort the president needs. Sincerely, William McKinley." Joe took the letter to the Henry Ford Museum and offered it to the curator. The curator said, "This letter is a fake." How did he know that?
2. The president's house was not called the White House until Theodore Roosevelt became president. In 1898, it was called the Executive Mansion.

Who won the race?

1. Two identical cars are at a stop light and the drivers agree to have a race to the next light. Car A has the A/C on the stereo blasting and the windows up. Car B has the A/C off, a talk show on the radio and the windows down. Which car will win the race?
2. Based on this information, the winning car should be car B because the A/C will take a lot of power away from the engine from car A. However, the cars computer will shut down the A/C in car A once the driver floors the gas pedal. The open windows now produce enough drag in car B to allow car A to win.

Is this possible?

1. In 1992 Bill is 13 years old. In 1999 Bill is 6 years old. How can that be? (hint: Bill isn't his real name.)
2. This could only happen if we are looking at 1992 B.C. (or, if we are politically correct B.C.E.)

Do you know these men?

1. What do the following people have in common besides being deceased? Ulysses S. Grant, Rudyard Kipling, Woodrow Wilson, Grover Cleveland and Calvin Coolidge. (hint: they are not all presidents.)
2. They are best known by using their middle names. Grant dropped his first name, Hiram. This left him with his middle name Ulysses. He added the "S" for Simpson later in life, but often went by Sam, which he picked up at West Point. The others all swapped ordinary names for funkier middle names:

Joseph Rudyard Kipling, Thomas Woodrow Wilson, Stephen Grover Cleveland and John Calvin Coolidge.

A conversational mystery

1. A man and a woman are driving around town on a nice sunny day. Every time they stop for a red light, they turn toward each other and have a conversation. When the light turns green, the conversation abruptly ends and they drive down the road until the next red light. This continues until they reach their destination. The car is not excessively loud, there's no background noise, and they don't have the radio on. Why do they converse only at red lights?
2. Their conversation is limited to red lights because they are both using sign language.

Can you get exactly 2 gallons without measuring?

1. You are out camping with 30 of your friends (sound familiar?). You are going to make pancakes for everyone in the morning, so you check the label on the pancake mix and calculate that you will need 2 gallons of water to make the entire mix. So, you go to the well to get the water and you have no measuring devise. At the well, there are two jugs, one says 13 gallons and the other says 7 gallons. How do you come back with exactly 2 gallons without fetching another container or making any extra trips to the well?
2. First, fill the 7-gallon container, then pour it into the 13-gallon jug. Do it again. You now have one gallon left in the 7-gallon jug. Empty the 13-gallon jug and pour the one gallon into it. Now fill the 7-gallon jug and pour it into the 13-gallon jug.

Do this again. You now have 2 gallons of water in the 7-gallon jug. Got it?

Stranded on a deserted island.

1. You are stranded on a deserted island that is 10 miles long and 100 yards wide. It is completely covered with grass and an occasional palm tree. There is a sheer drop-off all around the island. It is 500 feet down onto sharp rocks and shark-infested waters. In the center of the island you discovered an abandoned grass hut with the following things in it: a case of canned Beany-weenies, a case of bottled water, a poster of Ginger from *Gilligan's Island*, a flashlight, a box of matches and a blanket. That first night, you are awakened by a loud clash of thunder. Lightning has struck the far end of the island, about 5 miles away, setting the grass on fire. A breeze is blowing toward you at a rate of 2 miles an hour. How do you save yourself?
2. Face away from the fire. Then take the matches and light up the poster of Ginger to start another fire that will burn away from you. After it has burned a mile or so, move the beanie-weenies and water to a burned-out area for your consumption while you use the flashlight to signal airplanes that will surely come to take pictures of the burning island. You better pray that it doesn't rain.

You'll never get this one without cheating or reading the answer before you guess an answer. Good luck.

1. Two Bedouins are crossing the desert on their camels. It's early in the morning when they come across a suitcase in the sand that is partially open. There are no tracks of any kind surrounding

it. They look at the suitcase and see western-style clothing, so they move on. A little while longer they find another suitcase in the sand. Same thing as before. It's open and clothes are strewn about and no tracks anywhere. A little while later they find a video camera. Later still they find shoes, hats, pants, shirts all scattered in the sand. Finally, they see a man in his underwear lying face down in the sand holding a piece of straw. Obviously, he is dead. What happened?

2. The man was part of a party that was trying to make a trip across the desert in a hot air balloon. As they began to lose altitude, they began to throw off their suitcases and everything else. Finally, they said, "We are going to crash; someone's got to go?" They stripped off a few pieces from the basket they were riding in, hastily pulled straws and this poor guy had the short straw and had to jump.

Do you know your bicycles?

1. Back in the 1800's, the common form of bicycle was called the ordinary. This bike had a huge front wheel and a small rear wheel and the rider sat quite high. The common accident of this bicycle was called the header. It sent the rider over the handlebars and could cause death. To popularize cycling, something called the Safety Bike was developed, which had two wheels of the same size, a chain drive and many features we see on bikes today. But the safety bike didn't catch on at first. It was considered ugly, inefficient and uncomfortable. What made the safety bike desirous to the general public was an invention of a veterinarian in Belfast, Ireland. He patented an accessary the made the Ordinary obsolete. What was the name of the veterinarian and what did he patent?

2. The problem with both the Ordinary and the Safety bicycles were the hard rubber tires that made the ride very rough and uncomfortable. The veterinarian's name was John Dunlop and he invented the pneumatic tire.

Let's try math again.

1. A man and a boy wearing baseball caps at the local McDonalds are writing some numbers on a napkin. They are 2.1, 4.2, 3.0, 3.2. Then it is totaled at 13.2. They leave McDonalds and leave the napkin on a table when you walk by on your way to get another fill-up on your soda. You, being the math whiz that you are, realize that the sum totals 12.5. You think those two were morons with the wrong answer. Actually, they were right. What kind of calculations were they doing?
2. The man and the boy were actually the coach and the pitcher of a little league team and they were counting up the amount of innings the boy had pitched. Since baseball innings are measured in thirds, 4.2 is four and two-thirds of an inning. Go ahead, recheck the math.

Building a better fan belt.

1. In 1936, Europe is on the brink of war. In a secret location, German officers are gathered around a table with the designers of a new personnel carrier. As they went over every detail one officer asks the engineer, "How long will the fan belt last?" The engineer said, "30- to 40-thousand kilometers." The officer said, "Not good enough, we need at least 60,000." The engineer said, "No problem, just take off the belt and flip it over to get 60,000." The officer says, "That's unacceptable, we can't

ask soldiers to change the fan belts on the battlefield." So, the engineers came up with a clever design. They don't alter the material of the belt in any way, yet they satisfy the new requirement. What did they do?
2. The engineers figured out how to run the belt on both sides. They lengthen the belt, twisted it into an 8. This allows it to run on the inside and outside at the same time and double the length of time before it needs to be replaced.

Try this trick to find your friends.

1. Jim Wood was at the airport where his wife just left on a flight to visit her mother. While having a drink at the bar he sees his old college room-mate going to catch a plane. He went to go see him but lost him in the crowd. He couldn't remember his name but wanted to at least say hello and find out how he is doing. Jim knew he lived somewhere in the south so he went to the kiosk to check on flights. That's when he had an idea. Two minutes later he was reunited with his friend. What did he do?
2. He went to the customer service desk and had himself paged. Two minutes later his old friend was there to say hello.

The greatest invention during WWII.

1. During World War II, a small group of British scientists worked in a secret laboratory. They made a discovery that will greatly aid the Allied efforts against the Germans. But they needed some money to develop this product but they could not get the British government to help. So, they left Britain and went to America and had to smuggle their invention into the U.S.

in their clothing to not arouse suspicion. What invention were they hiding?

2. One of the greatest causes of death during war is getting an infection from wounds. These scientists had invented reproducible penicillin. This strain of penicillin mold could be grown in a lab. So, they rubbed this into their clothes and after they arrived they scraped it off.

If you don't know this one, pay attention, it could be helpful someday.

1. Meck Polk was taking a flight to Timbuktu for a badly needed vacation. At the airport, he boards an old DC 3 and is a little confused about why this plane is still in service. After boarding the plane, he decides to befriend some of the passengers but soon realizes no one speaks English. After a 15 hour flight the plane finally lands in Timbuktu but it is past midnight and there is no one there to greet him. He tries to get a cab but no one speaks English. Then Meck sees a woman from the plane and he knows she speaks English. How did he know that?
2. The woman from the plane was not a passenger, Instead, she was the pilot, and all pilots who fly internationally must speak English.

Well wise guys, how's your math?

1. A landscaper came home one night and his wife said to him, "Did you have a rough day?" He said," Oh yah, I planted trees today: five rows of four trees each." She said, "Wow, that makes twenty trees, no wonder you look so tired." He said, "Oh no, it was only ten trees." OK wise guys, how did he plant ten trees

in five rows of four each. Music sounds as you wise guys grab your calculators. Hint, a calculator will not help.
2. You were tricked if you thought this was a simple math problem. It is actually a geometry problem. The landscaper planted the trees in the shape of a five-pointed star. Draw a star, then put a tree at the intersection of each line and one at each vertex. You get five rows of four trees each.

Did you find your hat?

1. At the end of the Little League season, the coach has a barbeque at his house and twenty-five kids show up. The coach says that nobody can wear their hat at the barbeque so twenty hats are thrown into a pile and the kids go about eating hotdogs and deep-fried Twinkies and have a good time. At the end of party, they all reach into the pile of hats and grab a hat at random and puts in on his head. What is the probability that 24 out of 25 of these kids get their original hat back?
2. The answer has to be zero because if 24 kids got the right hat, then the 25th kid as to get the right hat too.

The lady and the tiger.

1. A king designs a series of tests for men vying to marry his beautiful daughter. After a dozen contests the final challenge is to draw a slip of paper from a bucket. There are two slips of paper is the bucket: one says "the Lady" and the other says "The Tiger." If a suitor chooses the lady slip, he wins her hand. If he chooses the tiger slip, he is thrown into the tiger cage. Suiters come and go and the tiger gets fat. One day prince charming arrives. He dazzles the princess by completing all of the tests in

record fashion. It was now time to draw a slip from the bucket. The princess likes this young man so she tells him that her father is a cheater. She warns him that both pieces of paper say "The Tiger." The prince tells her not to worry. How does he win her hand without cheating or exposing the king's treachery?

2. The prince draws out a slip and declares that he has won the princess's hand. He then swallows the slip of paper. If challenged he can show that the remaining slip says "The Tiger." The king must accept the outcome because if he protests, he exposes his own treachery.

You're not as smart as you think?

1. As you drive through the parking lot at the movie theater looking for a place to park, you notice a car with an interesting license plate. It reads TAN 270. What is the make of this car?
2. TAN 270 refers to the tangent of 270, and the tangent of 270 is undefined or infinite. So, did you get it? Really? The car is an Infiniti.

Here' an easy one.

1. A lady brings her car into the car dealership and complains that a fuse in her car is blowing out repeatedly. A mechanic comes to look at the problem and when he opens the door of the car he knows immediately what the problem is. He sees something on the dashboard that explains the problem. What is on the dashboard? (clue- it is not a light or sign).
2. There is a compass on the dashboard. The short circuit is disturbing the surrounding electromagnetic field, causing the compass to spin wildly. There is a shorted wire in the dashboard near the compass.

What happened to this car?

1. Elijah Fawbusch bought a brand-new Toyota Camry and he went out and bought a few accessories. He bought a glue on digital clock, floor mats and fuzzy dice to hang from his rearview mirror. The next day the engine won't crank. After several attempts, he finally gets it going. This happens every time he tries to drive his car. So, he takes the car back to the dealer to complain. The dealer immediately realizes what is wrong. Which of the three items Fawbusch added to his car was responsible for the difficulty in starting the car?
2. Did you just guess one of the above? So, do you know why? If you picked the fuzzy dice, you need to get some help. The Camry has a manual shift, and like many stick shift cars it has a switch that disables the starter motor if you don't depress the clutch. Fawbusch had installed thick floor mats that slid around the clutch pedal and sometimes it was not depressed well enough to start the car. Now the floor mats are in the back seat where they belong.

This one will stump you?

1. When you have been asked a question, like many in this book, and you don't know the answer, have you ever said, "I'm stumped." Or "that one stumped me?" Where does this term come from?
2. Back in the early days of the founding of the United States, farmers often had to clear trees off their land so that they could plant their crops. After the trees were cut down the stumps had to be removed. The larger stumps were sometimes too difficult

to remove and were left in place and prevented growing crops there. What this did to the farmers literally stumped them.

Do you need a haircut?

1. You are in need of a haircut in a town that has only two barber shops. You go to the first shop and see the barber is unshaven, dirty and has a lousy haircut. So, you go to the second barber shop and see a nice clean shop and the barber has a great haircut. Which barber should you choose to give you a haircut?
2. You should have chosen the messy one. Since there are only two barbers in town the dirty barber gave the neat barber his stylish cut. And why is the other guy's shop so neat? Because he has no customers. The dirty barber is too busy to clean up his shop.

Can you make 5 feet long into 4 feet long?

1. A man is waiting at the bus stop with his brand new 5-foot-long fishing pole. When the bus arrives, the bus driver tells him he can't bring the fishing pole onto the bus because nothing longer than 4 feet is allowed. So, the man goes back to the store and without altering the rod, breaking it or collapsing it, he returns to catch the next bus. When the bus arrives, he gets right on and heads for home. What did he do to the fishing rod?
2. He bought a three foot by four feet box and put the fishing pole in the box diagonally. And you think you are wise.

Don't you love being so smart?

1. Albert Sailhorst finally got rid of that old pickup parked in front of his house. A junk dealer gave him $25 for it and then sent it to a crusher. It was turned into a 3-by-3-by-3-foot solid cube

of rust weighing 3000 pounds. It was shipped to Chicago and put on a barge with a hundred other cubes of rust. On the way across Lake Michigan this cube falls overboard. Assuming that water cannot escape from the lake, does the water level go up, go down or stay the same?
2. When the 3000-pound cube is in the barge, it's displacing its weight in water. A cubic foot of water weighs 62.4 pounds, so the barge displaces 48 cubic feet (3000 divided by 62.4 is about 48). When the cube sinks, it displaces an amount of water equal to its volume. Since it's a 3-foot cube, that's 27 cubic feet. So, the water level goes down about 21 cubic feet (48 minus 27 equals 21).

Did you know this?

1. Old broken-down cars are often called a Jalopy. So where did this term come from?
2. Back in the 1920's worn-out American cars were shipped to Mexico, a practice that still occurs today. The typical destination in Mexico was Jalapa which is pronounced ha-la-pa in Spanish. The longshoremen who were putting the junkers on the boats mispronounced the name of the town. That eventually turned into jalopy.

Flapping chickens

1. Eugene Sullivan is a chicken rancher. He has put 1000 pounds of chickens in his truck that weighs 2 tons (4,000 lbs.). The total weight of the truck is now 5000 pounds plus the 250 pounds that Sullivan weighs. He comes to a bridge with a sign that says "Maximum Weight 5000 Pounds." So, he revs up the engine,

bangs on the truck to get the chickens flying, thus making the truck lighter, and speeds across the bridge. Will he make it to the other side?

2. The downward air pressure exerted by the flapping wings of the chickens is at least equal to the weight of the chickens. Otherwise, how would they fly? So, he's not going to make.

Losing your marbles?

1. You have three cloth bags that have ten marbles in each bag. The bags are labeled "white", "black" and "mixed" but these labels are incorrect. How many marbles do you need to take out of any bag to figure out which bag is really the white bag, really the black bag and rally the mixed bag?
2. You only need to take out one marble from the mixed bag. If it is white, then you know this is the white bag. Since the other bags are labeled incorrectly, just reverse what each one says on the label.

CHAPTER 4

THE MEANINGS OF YOGI-ISMS

Q. What is a Yogi-ism?
A. Something Yogi Berra said that made perfect sense to him, but might not make sense to you.

Q. Why should we care what Yogi Berra said?
A. Here are some possible answers:

1. What he says is funny.
2. What he says is stupid.
3. Anyone named Yogi must have wisdom.
4. He is one of the great sages of history.

Q. Who is Yogi Berra?
A. Here is the Wikipedia answer:

Lawrence Peter "Yogi" Berra (May 12, 1925 – September 22, 2015) was an American professional **baseball catcher**, who later took on the roles of **manager** and **coach**. He played 19 seasons in **Major League Baseball** (MLB) (1946–1963, 1965), all but the last for the **New York Yankees**. He was an 18-time **All-Star** and won 10 **World Series** championships as a player—more than any other player in MLB history.

[2] Berra had a career **batting average** of .285, while hitting 358 **home runs** and 1,430 **runs batted in**. He is one of only six players to win the **American League Most Valuable Player Award** three times. He is widely regarded as one of the greatest catchers in baseball history,[3] and was elected to the **Baseball Hall of Fame** in **1972**.

Q. That's quite impressive, but what about the Yogi-isms?
A. Yogi was often asked questions by the press to various things about baseball or life in general. He said many profound things. Let's take a look at what he has said with what he really meant when he said it.

1. "You can observe a lot just by watching."
   Meaning: observing while sleeping has not worked out so well.

2. "The future ain't what it used to be."
   Meaning: some of that future is now the past and didn't turn out so well.

3. "Half the lies they tell about me aren't true."
   Meaning: but the other half of the lies are true.

4. "When you get to a fork in the road, take it." Meaning: Maybe there is a complete place setting up the road. Start collecting your dishes a few pieces at a time.

5. "Ninety percent of this game is half mental." Meaning: That makes the other half of the game ten percent physical. And statistics never lie half the time.

6. "I really didn't say everything I said."
   Meaning: some ventriloquist must have said it.

7. "We have a good time together, even when we're not together."
   Meaning: we have a better when we're not together.

8. "If you don't know where you're going, you might end up someplace else."
   Meaning: none needed, this is pure wisdom.

9. "It gets late early around here."
   Meaning: and in the morning, it gets early later too. Yogi seems to go to bed early and sleep in.

10. "A nickel ain't worth a dime anymore." Meaning: like today a dollar can't buy a nickels worth.

11. "I usually take a two-hour nap from one to four". Meaning: I'm such a restless sleeper when I nap so leave me alone.

12. "Slump? I ain't in no slump… I just ain't hitting." Meaning: Ah, Yogi, I hate to tell you, but, ah, not hitting is a slump.

13. "No one goes there nowadays, it's too crowded." Meaning: I won't go there nowadays because all of you are there.

14. "Always go to other people's funerals, otherwise they won't come to yours."
    Meaning: No one is coming to my funeral because all of my friends have died.

15. "We made too many wrong mistakes."
    Meaning: What we did right we did on purpose, what we did wrong was mistakes.

16. "How can you think and hit at the same time?"
    Meaning: I obviously have a problem when you want me to think when I bat. So, stop asking me questions.

17. "All pitchers are liars or crybabies."
    Meaning: According to you pitchers, you make the team win the games; when in reality it is the opposite.

18. "Even Napoleon had his Watergate."
    Meaning: Every baseball player sometimes has a very bad day. He really didn't know his history very well.

19. "Bill Dickey is learning me his experience."
    Meaning: Yogi was learning from Bill Dickey, just like you are learning from Yogi.

20. "It was impossible to get a conversation going, everybody was talking too much."
    Meaning: Obviously Yogi didn't have anything important to say or they would have listened to him. I think they had already heard too many yogi-isms.

21. "I'm so ugly. I never saw anyone hit with his face."
    Meaning: Apparently Yogi got his good looks by getting hit in the face with a baseball a few times.

22. (On the 1973 Mets) "We were overwhelming underdogs."
    Meaning: Now think about this yogi-ism, think hard. He is saying they were a really bad team, really bad.

23. "The towels were so thick there I could hardly close my suitcase."
    Meaning: The towels were so nice at this place I didn't have enough room in my suitcase to steel more than one, what a bummer.

24. "I'm not going to buy my kids an encyclopedia. Let them walk to school like I did."
Meaning: As long as the kids have to walk to school, they will be able to get as smart as me. He probably didn't know how to ride an encyclopedia.

25. "In baseball, you don't know nothing."
Meaning: Boy is that the truth, just look at the high intellectual bar placed on these yogi-isms.

26. "I never blame myself when I'm not hitting. I just blame the bat and if it keeps up, I change bats. After all, if I know it isn't my fault that I'm not hitting, how can I get mad at myself?"
Meaning: We get it. Your logic is perfect.

27. "It ain't the heat, it's the humility."
Meaning: It's not the heat or the humidity, it's the pressure from the fans that expect you to have more humility.

28. "I don't know (if they were men or women fans running naked across the field). They had bags over their heads."
Meaning: Sure, that's where everyone's eyes were during the incident.

29. "I'm a lucky guy and I'm happy to be with the Yankees. And I want to thank everyone for making this night necessary.
Meaning: Yogi, it wasn't necessary, we just wanted to show our respect.

30. "Pair up in threes."
Meaning: Get into groups of three. He thinks any group of any size is a pair.

31. "We have deep depth."
    Meaning: We have three or more guys at every position. Maybe ten at every position.

32. "Congratulations. I knew the record would stand until it was broken."
    Meaning: Must have been an easy record to break. Next time make the record harder to break.

33. "Why buy good luggage, you only use it when you travel."
    Meaning: I'm not wasting money on expensive luggage unless I can get more towels in them.

34. "If the people don't want to come out to the ballpark, nobody's going to stop them."
    Meaning: It's not worth stopping people that aren't coming.

35. "If you ask me anything I don't know, I'm not going to answer."
    Meaning: That's a good idea.

36. "I wish everybody had the drive he (Joe DiMaggio) had. He never did anything wrong on the field. I'd never seen him dive for a ball, everything was a chest-high catch, and he never walked off the field."
    Meaning: He was lucky every ball was hit right at him. I've had to run all over the field, and sometimes dive at the ball, to make a catch because nobody ever hit right to me.

37. "Little League baseball is a very good thing because it keeps the parents off the streets."
    Meaning: Nothing worse than parents running all over the streets. They need to be with their kids.

38. "Mickey Mantle was a very good golfer, but we weren't allowed to play golf during the season; only at spring training."
Meaning: I wish we could have played golf in the off-season, but the management said we had to play golf between spring training games, what a bummer.

39. "You don't have to swing hard to hit a home run. If you got the timing, it'll go."
Meaning: I don't hit too many homeruns because I try to hit the ball to hard.

40. "Take it with a grin of salt."
Meaning: I always like smiling salt.

41. "He hits from both sides of the plate. He's amphibious."
Meaning: Are we talking baseball or frogs here? What did Mickey Mantle say about that?

42. "You better cut the pizza in four pieces because I'm not hungry enough to eat six."
Meaning: Yah, four slices is less than eating six. And I bet your diet is working well.

43. "You wouldn't have won if we'd beaten you."
Meaning: We lost because you won. But we never lose, we just get beat.

44. "I tell the kids, somebody's gotta win, somebody's gotta lose. Just don't fight about it. Just try to get better."
Meaning; Actually, some good advice. Way to go Yogi.

45. "Never answer an anonymous letter."
    Meaning: Why not, don't you know where to send it?

46. "You've got to be very careful if you don't know where you are going, because you might not get there."
    Meaning: If you don't know where you're going you won't ever get there.

47. "I can see how he (Sandy Koufax) won twenty-five games. What I don't understand is how he lost five."
    Meaning: Simple math Yogi; the other team scored more runs in those 5 games.

48. "I'm lucky. Usually you're dead to get your own museum, but I'm still alive to see mine."
    Meaning: Yes, you are lucky to live long enough to see all your stuff put in an organized collection.

49. "If the world were perfect, it wouldn't be."
    Meaning: If the world were perfect, we would never have any yogi-isms.

50. "If I didn't make it in baseball, I won't have made it workin'. I didn't like to work."
    Meaning: Good thing you liked baseball because we know you didn't like to work.

51. "It's like déjà vu all over again."
    Meaning: That's what we thought as we read these yogi-isms.

52. "A lot of guys go, 'Hey, Yog, say a Yogi-ism.' I tell 'em, 'I don't know any.' They want me to make one up. I don't make 'em up. I don't even know when I say it. They're the truth. And it is the truth. I don't know."

Meaning: Yes, all yogi-isms are the truth.

CHAPTER 5

THE HEART OF THE ISSUE

Q. Who should I vote for? The guy who plays like he is poor but actually is a millionaire and owns three houses, or the dude who has billions of dollars and has a commercial on every TV show?

A. Ask two questions- 1. What do I get? And 2. What's does he get? If the answer to the first question is something you want, like world peace, but you are only going to get free food, look for a third choice. If they get power and more wealth instead of world peace, then look for a third choice. Intangible things are more valuable than free things. Besides if they want you to have free things, why don't they just buy them for you with their own money?

Q. Have we ever had a president who wasn't rich or became rich after being president?

A. Only one comes to my mind, Lincoln. I think his wife had something to do about that.

Q. What did you learn in kindergarten that is still true today?

A. That the dog next door was B-I-N-G-O and that the wheels on the bus did go round and round.

Q. Is time male or female?

A. Obviously it is female because it waits for no man.

Q. The doctor says that I need to drink more water. Does that mean that I need to drink less whiskey?
A. No, of course not. You are to add ice to your drinks.

Q. During Lent every fast food place is hustling fish sandwiches. So, who has the best sandwich?
A. It must be Culver's because they are the only one who have this guy in a boat catching them one by one.

Q. What object made by man first broke the sound barrier?
A. Some of you may think it was Chuck Yeager flying the X-15 or maybe how fast your mother slapped your brother the first time he used a cuss word. Both are wrong, but your mother may come in second. It was actually the whip. The crack you hear is the tip of the whip breaking the sound barrier.

Q. If the Wicked Witch of the West melts in water, how did she ever bathe?
A. She had to go to the dry cleaners.

Q. What three things would you bring to a deserted Island?
A. Only one thing really matters. Bring a boat.

Q. Is a fly without wings a walk?
A. No, more like a dive and a crash.

Q. When something fades in the sunlight, where did the colors go?
A. They are still there. Look deeper into the material or even onto the back where the colors should even be brighter. While you are there do some cleaning so we can see them better.

Q. Where are the germs that cause 'good' breath?
A. You don't have any.

Q. The sergeant told me I could go to town after dark. When is that, after sunset?
A. Don't be silly. After dark comes light, therefore it is after sunrise.

Q. Why do you need an appointment to see a psychic?
A. You don't, she knows when you're coming. She even knows you're going to give her a $50 tip. You better get going because your appointment is in an hour from now.

Q. Can you hear yourself think?
A. I can't but I am sure you can.

Q. What happens if you go on a survival course - and you don't pass?
A. You get a nice burial marker made of rocks.

Q. What happens when you swallow your pride?
A. Many people often choke on it. Some even die.

Q. What if someone died in the living room?
A. We could hold a wake without having to leave the room. Probably should put away the chicken wings that he died from.

Q. Why do fat chance and slim chance mean the same thing?
A. It is a play on words. Fat chance makes you think you have a better chance than a slim chance when in reality you have no chance in hell.

Q. What does no chance in hell mean?
A. It means that even if you die you won't win.

Q. If a person suffered from amnesia and then was cured would they remember that they forgot?
A. Yes. Your wisdom is so perfect.

Q. Why do they write, "May contain traces of peanuts or other kind of nuts" on peanut butter jars?
A. Because there may be traces of nuts in the peanut butter. This is not a problem. Be alert for jars that may say the following: "May contain traces of chicken feathers, mouse dung, toe nail clippings, beaver semen, fumunda cheese or bull shit."

Q. What is fumunda cheese?
A. That gooey substance found from under something. Example: that greenish substance found between your toes.

Q. Why is it so difficult to solve a redneck murder?
A. First of all, the DNA will be the same and there usually are no dental records.

Q. What four-letter word should never be said by a doctor during surgery?
A. OOPS.

Q. What is the rule of thumb?
A. Back in the middle ages there was a law that said you could not beat your wife with a stick thinker than your thumb. The sergeant uses this rule when you get your beef or pork ration. The HQ staff discards thicker portions so no one gets more than anyone else.

Q. What does the word "golf" mean?
A. Originally it was a Scottish game played only by men. The posting of GOLF, which means Gentlemen Only Ladies Forbidden, often

appears in various city parks to signify that if you are not a gentleman you should stay out of the park. Please note your place when you see the word golf.

Q. Is it possible to lick your eyebrow?
A. No, but I can see that several of the men don't believe this and may be seen in camp trying to prove the answer wrong.

Q. Do the kings in a deck of cards represent anybody in history?
A. Yes, the spade is King David, the hearts is Charlemagne, the clubs is Alexander the Great and the diamonds is Julius Caesar.

Q. Who does the joker represent?
A. You.

Q. I think you just tried to lick your eyebrows.
A. Yes you did.

Q. If you multiply 111,111,111 X 111,111,111 what will you get?
A. This is something you really need to know. Most of you have already taken a calculator for the answer, which is 12,345,678,987,654,321.

Q. Statues of horses take many different poses. Is there a reason for that?
A. Yes, if the horse has both front legs in the air it means that the person on the horse died in battle. If the horse has one front leg in the air the person died as a result of wounds received in battle. If the horse has all four legs on the ground it means that the person died of natural causes. If the horse is lying down it means that the horse died in battle. Bird shit on the statue means this man is still disliked even today.

Q. Most boat owners name their boats. What is the most popular name for a boat?
A. Obsession.

Q. If you were to spell out numbers, how far would you have to go until you could find the letter "A"?
A. I can see you now, thinking through all the numbers as words. Did you get to one thousand yet?

Q. How many cars were wrecked in a single scene of the Blues Brothers movie?
A. 52, but maybe you should watch it again and do a recount.

Q. Where does the term honeymoon come from?
A. In ancient Babylon a bride's father was supposed to supply his son-in-law all the mead he could drink for the first month after the wedding. Mead is a beer made from honey. Apparently, women were ugly back then.

Q. What is so scary about living in a retirement facility?
A. All the old ladies running around with faded and sagging tattoos and pierced navels.

Q. When will I know that I am middle aged?
A. When you choose your cereal for the fiber and not the toy.

Q. Is it true that water contains E. coli?
A. Yes, E. coli is found in our feces as small amounts of it come from the water we drink. Be advised that any liquor, wine or beer does not have E. coli as it has been boiled, filtered and or fermented before it is bottled.

Q. What is better for me; wine or water?
A. Remember that wine equals health and water equals poop. Therefore, it is better to drink wine and talk stupid than to drink water and be full of shit.

Q. Is laughing good exercise?
A. Yes, it is like jogging on the inside.

Q. Should I be afraid of getting wrinkles?
A. No, because they don't hurt.

Q. What can a friend do for me when I am sad?
A. Help get you drunk and plot revenge against the sorry bastard that made you sad.

Q. Can kids in the back-seat cause accidents?
A. You have it backwards. Accidents in the backseat cause kids.

Q. Why don't people like the IRS?
A. When it comes to money, see what THE IRS spells.

Q. What happened to Preparation A through G?
A. No one was interested in a cream that causes itching, irritable bowels, anal leakage, hives, ulcers, lymphoma, leukemia, and in 40% of test trials, death.

Q. If cows laughed would milk come out of their noses?
A. Only if they were drinking milk. Since you have this problem, Captain Scott suggests that you clean out your nose by laughing and drinking soapy water.

Q. Why do they put pictures of criminals up in the Post Office?
A. Interesting point since the criminals probably stay away from the post office. It would be a better idea to put the criminal's pictures on the stamps so the mailman can look for them while he delivers the mail.

Q. Do Lipton Tea employees take coffee breaks?
A. You bet they do. Coffee helps get that nasty tea flavor out of your system.

Q. If lawyers are disbarred and clergymen are defrocked for breaking their oaths, do others suffer similar penalties?
A. Yes, electricians are delighted and dry cleaners are depressed.

Q. If it is true that we are here to help others, then what are others here for?
A. To piss us off with these stupid questions.

Q. If people from Poland are called Poles, then why aren't people from Holland called Holes?
A. Your logic is perfect. Ask some more questions so we can rate your I.Q. I think you are going to win a prize.

Q. Why do croutons come in airtight packages? Aren't they just stale bread to begin with?
A. Sure, but you want them fresh, don't you?

Q. What is life worth?
A. Life isn't worth much or you could trade it in for some needed cash. The labor of a life is worth more than life itself. In 1860 a strong field hand was worth $1000. Your labor is worth about 25 cents per day and your army pay is worth $11 a month. You should have asked, "What is death worth?"

Q. What is death worth?
A. Nothing unless you buy "life" insurance. Many policies pay over one million dollars. It isn't worth buying life insurance for yourself. Instead, buy several policies on your friends and then plan their deaths.

Q. How many things does a man have in the bathroom?
A. Six: toothbrush, toothpaste, shaving cream, razor, a bar of soap and a towel.

Q. How many things does a woman have in the bathroom?
A. The number varies but averages at about 337. A man would not be able to identify more than 20 of those.

Q. What is the best thing about being a man?
A. The world is your urinal.

Q. What is a planet?
A. A body of earth surrounded by a sky.

Q. What's worse than being in a rut?
A. Being in a grave. It's much deeper.

Q. My wife never lets me have the last word. What can I do?
A. You can get the last word in. Just apologize.

Q. Why haven't we heard about UFOs very much lately?
A. Today everyone has a camera in their phone.

Q. What advise can you give me on how to make ends meet?
A. You should forget about making ends meet. The problem is that someone is always moving the ends.

Q. Have you heard the question "Do these jeans make my butt look fat?
A. Yes, and jeans do not have the ability to make you look any worse than you already are.

Q. Where can men over the age of 60 find younger women who are interested in them?
A. Try a bookstore and look for the fiction section.

Q. What can a man do while his wife is going through menopause?
A. Keep busy. If you are handy with tools, you can finish the basement. When you're done you will have a place to live.

Q. How can I avoid elderly wrinkles?
A. Take off your glasses.

Q. Is it common for the elderly to have problems with short-term memory storage?
A. Storing memory is not the problem. Retrieving it is the problem.

Q. What is the leading cause of diminished sex drive among senior citizens?
A. Nudity.

Q. Do elderly people ever "get lucky?"
A. Sure. Sometimes they find their parked car at the first place they look.

Q. Is it possible to have sex with a prostitute against her will?
A. Yes, it is called shoplifting.

Q. What is cured ham?
A. Apparently it is the meat from a hog that was once sick.

Q. Why do some people park their $50,000 car in the driveway when they have a garage?
A. Because the garage is being used to store tons of useless junk. This junk has much more meaning to them because in a few years they will sell the car and still have a garage full of junk.

Q. When can you trespass on people's property, knock on their door and make a non-negotiable demand that they fulfill?
A. Between 5 and 8 pm. on Halloween.

Q. Do you know the politically correct term for being lazy?
A. Yes, a selective participator.

Q. What two words rhyme but have opposite meanings?
A. Getting thinner and having more dinner.

Q. Would you say that a cookie jar is half full or half empty?
A. I would want to know who ate half my cookies.

Q. What was the last challenge that you won?
A. For me it was completing a fourteen-day diet in just two hours and twelve minutes.

Q. What rule do they break on Old McDonald's farm?
A. The I before E rule.

Q. When I fix something with duct tape, how do I know when I have used enough tape?
A. When you hear someone say, "is that enough duct tape?"

Q. Has McDonalds done anything to reduce the number of calories in their meals?
A. Absolutely, to reduce the calories on your supersized Big Mac meal McDonalds suggests you order a diet Coke with that.

Q. I don't feel like saying "Good Morning" every day when I meet people. What would you suggest I say instead?
A. Try saying "Here we go again." It's worked for me.

Q. Before there were sports drinks, what did athletes drink when they got dehydrated and thirsty?
A. It's still available and very inexpensive. It's called the garden hose.

Q. When does a person realize that they are getting old?
A. When they sit on the floor and then need help getting up.

Q. I get confused when I read food packages and they say what a serving size is. What am I supposed to do? Measure everything before I eat it?
A. Silly you. That is only the recommended size. The real portion size is what you say it is.

Q. What is the most challenging thing about marriage?
A. Trying to find the things your spouse moved.

Q. What is the best way to wash my hands?
A. Pretend that you just ate a lot of buffalo wings and your about to put on a white wedding dress. (Rented tuxedo for you ruffians)

Q. Who was the scariest person you ever knew?
A. My grade school principal, she looked just like Nancy Pelosi.

Q. What would be an ideal amount of weight to lose so I won't feel so fat?
A. You know you are there when you are able to finally reach inside the Pringles can.

Q. Is it true that going to sleep on Sunday night causes Monday to occur?
A. Your logic is perfect, so the answer is yes. You might want to try staying up all night on Sunday to prevent Monday from occurring.

Q. Can you guess what I have discovered to be the easiest thing in the world to do?
A. yes, get fat.

Q. Have you ever met someone who has plenty of energy, high moral principles and wants to fight crime?
A. Yes, I have. It sounds like a four-year-old wearing a batman cape.

Q. Have you ever said something funny instead of the right answer?
A. Because of some of your stupid questions, the answer is yes.

Q. Have you ever met someone who is doing something they are not qualified for?
A. Now that you mention it, yes, it is you.

Q. When the store clerk asks if I want my milk in a bag, should I do that?
A. Don't do that. It is very messy. You should leave the milk in the carton.

Q. What is the correct spelling for this name: Tom Cruise, Ted Cruz or Terry Crews?
A. We don't have an opinion on this. Perhaps the three of them should settle this question with a cage match.

Q. My wife has been missing for over a week. The police said I better plan for the worst. What should I do?
A. See if you can get her clothes back from the Salvation Army.

Q. I'm looking for something fun to do that is different, inexpensive and will be a load of laughs. What might you suggest I do?
A. Tomorrow take two witnesses with you and dress in a blue shirt and tan pants and go to Best Buy. Ask for the manager and then tell him that you quit.

Q. I don't think I can do that, do you have any other ideas?
A. Sure, dress up in a red polo shirt and Khaki pants and take two friends with you to the nearest State Farm Insurance Agency and turn in your resignation?

Q. How is any of this funny?
A. When you take two friends with you they will tell the rest of us how successful you were quitting a job you don't have. We think that will be funny.

Q. I hear there is a coin shortage. What is the cause of that?
A. I'm not sure about where you live, but in my area, all of my friends decided to clean up our language and started swear buckets.

Q. I have concerns about the decisions the government makes. Is there anything I can do?
A. You obviously are voting for the wrong people. Have you ever considered sending the government something to guide their decisions? We suggest you send them a new Magic 8 ball.

Q. Where is the best place to get really good fresh produce?
A. Down the block in my neighbor's garden. Really good stuff and cheap too.

Q. When does a person become old?
A. When they stop lying about their age and begin bragging about it.

Q. How do you make holy water?
A. Boil the hell out of it.

Q. Did you ever have someone ruin your day?
A. No one can ruin your day without your permission.

Q. What is the best way to escape my problems?
A. You can either decide to solve them or get drunk.

Q. Where do I need to go to register my complaints?
A. Sorry, yesterday was the deadline for complaints.

Q. My wife always wants to argue with me. What can I do?
A. You don't have to attend every argument you're invited to.

Q. What is the best way to relax?
A. With an idle mind.

Q. Laugh and the whole world laughs with you, but what if I cry?
A. You will need a tissue to blow your nose.

Q. I went to the social security office to sign up for benefits and when I couldn't produce an ID the lady said, "show me your chest." I thought it was strange but complied and she saw my gray chest hair and finished the application. Is this common practice?
A. Yes, in fact if you had dropped your pants you might have gotten disability too.

Q. How do I know if there is a curse on my marriage?
A. If you have video of your wedding vows go back and watch them. See if the exact words of the curse are said: "I now pronounce you man and wife."

Q. My wife's doctor said he doesn't like the way my wife looks, should I get a second opinion?
A. It is not necessary if she is a good cook and will have sex with you.

Q. Unnamed soldier asked Lt. Marsh: "I didn't sleep with my wife before marriage, did you?"
A. Marsh replied: "I'm not sure. What was her maiden name?"

Q. Is it unhealthy to hold my farts in and not let them go?
A. Of course it is. Let them go and let the rest of your friends tell you about your health.

Q. Why do dogs retrieve a ball when you throw it?
A. Dogs think you like to throw balls and it amuses them.

Q. Which letter is silent in the word "scent," the S or the C?
A. The S is silent. It is always the first letter when 2 consonants are together at the beginning of a word. Example: pneumonia and psycho and philharmonic. The P is silent in every case.

Q. Do twins ever not like their twin?
A. Rarely, usually after finding out that one of them was not planned.

Q. Why is the letter W, in English, called a double U? Shouldn't it be a double V?
A. It's a double U because it is a vowel.

Q. What is the fastest land mammal in the world?
A. Recent studies indicate that it is a toddler who was just asked by his father "what's in your mouth?"

Q. Did you know there is not one canary on the Canary Islands?
A. Yes, it's the same with the Virgin Islands- not one canary there either.

Q. Have you noticed how fast a child can pick up dropped things?
A. Oh yah, now I have to decide if I need it anymore before I spend the effort to pick it up.

Q. Sometimes my eyes hurt after drinking coffee. What is the cause of that?
A. You forgot to take the spoon out of your cup.

Q. I have a hard time remembering what day it is. What advise do you have for me?
A. Arrange your underwear with the day of the week written on them and don't get dressed in the dark.

Q. Is it true that Illinois has a department called the Sandwich Police?
A. Yes, and the way you make sandwiches you better stay out of Sandwich, Illinois.

Q. What do you consider to be the most important technological innovation?
A. Most people would say the automobile or perhaps the miniaturization of the computer so you can wear it on your wrist like Dick Tracy. But for you it is the gravy boat. You can't live without it.

Q. What is one of the most enjoyable things about sitting around the campfire?
A. Seeing a bunch of 50+ year-olds pretend to have the body of a 28-year-old and have the mind of a 12-year-old.

Q. How can just one person, like myself, save ten trees.
A. Try using the receipts you get from fast-food, big box and drugstores in your fireplace this winter instead of wood. That's about 10 trees per year.

Q. Do you know what you will never hear anyone say at a pizza party?
A. For most people you will never hear anyone say the crust is the best part of the pizza, except for you.

Q. I've heard that cardiovascular exercise will help prolong your life. Is this true?
A. We have consulted the visiting Chinese Doctor at the prestigious University of Pidgeon Ridge Medical School, Dr. Chin Not Wong. Here is what he has to say about that: "Heart only good for so many beats, and that it. Don't waste on exercise. Everything wear out eventually. Speeding up heart not make you live longer; it like saying extend life of car by driving faster. Want to live longer? Take nap.

Q. Over the years, what has caused you the most pain?
A. The inability of the bed post and my right big toe to get along.

Q. Throughout your lifetime, have you had more accomplishments or stories to tell.
A. My biggest accomplishment has been to tell many true stories, most are sad but funny because I'm not very intelligent.

Q. Do you have any ideas how to keep burglars away from my house?
A. If you have kids in college, post the tuition bills on your front door.

Q. I saw a car with an elderly couple drive by with a sign in the window that said "just married." I think that was rather bold for elderly newlyweds. What do you think?
A. That couple has been married for 40 years, thus the sign of lost bliss.

Q. What should I do if I think someone is following me when I driving to the grocery store?
A. Drive like you are in a James Bond movie. That should get rid of them.

Q. My teenage son asked me to explain taxes. What would be a good way to show him what taxes are like.
A. Take him to Pancheros and make him pay for a burrito. Then you eat 41% of it and tell him he gets the rest.

Q. How do I know when I have enough money to be considered rich?
A. You know you are rich when your dog has a dog.

Q. What does it mean when a woman says "What."
A. She isn't asking you to repeat what you said, she is giving you a chance to change your response.

Q. Some of my friends say I am immature. I am 55 years old and think I am as mature as anyone else. What do you think?
A. Stop going to your friend's houses at night leaving pink flamingos in their yards.

Q. Some drivers seam to ignore my horn when I want to get their attention. What can I do?
A. Start carrying fireworks in your car. It has worked for me.

Q. How do I keep my kids from running out to the ice cream truck when it comes down my street?
A. Tell them that when the music is playing, they are out of ice cream.

Q. What is a newborn baby?
A. A redundant statement.

Q. What does a rodeo teach people about life?
A. That some people do stupid things with wild animals. Which of the things you see at a rodeo would you like to do? How about at a bull fight? If you chose an answer, I rest my case.

Q. In this digital age I think it is a good idea for students to learn how to write in cursive. Is there anything else that you think they should learn that is being forgotten?
A. Yes, how to use a rotary phone and how to read the hands on a clock. It also wouldn't hurt them to put away their video games and play a game of pong.

Q. Is there anything that still fits you that you haven't worn in ten years?
A. Only my hat.

Q. What would make a politician more interesting to watch?
A. If liars pants really did catch on fire.

Q. What is the cause of wind?
A. Recent research has determined that wind can be generated by eating a large helping of beans and cooked cabbage and wash it down with beer. Then wait 30 minutes or jump up and down for 10 minutes. There may be some rumbling before you hear the wind break.

Q. I don't understand the controversy over Roe v. Wade. Could you explain it to me?
A. It mainly has to do with whether you want to get your pants wet and how deep the water is. Deep water you will row and shallow water you will wade.

Q. Why is it that some people never seem to be embarrassed?
A. Because you can't be embarrassed if you don't care what people think.

Q. If a woman says "I'm not mad at you," what does she really mean?
A. It has the same meaning as the dentist saying "You won't feel a thing."

Q. My teenage son seems to be living in another world. What can I do?
A. Start recording the things that he does that seem alien to you. Here is an example of alien things you may observe: pouring milk into the bowl before the cereal, eating soft butter with a spoon like ice cream, thoroughly covering ice cream with pepper before eating it or refusing to eat at McDonalds because he prefers humus.

Q. What was the most pleasurable trip you ever took?
A. The last time I took my mother-in-law to the airport.

Q. I heard that you have been in love with the same woman for 50 years. What is your secret to this long relationship?
A. My wife has never found out about it.

Q. What are the three words a woman never wants to hear when she is making love?
A. Honey, I'm Home.

Q. My wife lost her credit card and I decided not to tell the credit card company. Do you know why?
A. I have a pretty good idea. The thief probably spends less than your wife.

Q. I always see you at the shopping mall holding hands with your wife. That's so sweet. Why do you always do that?
A. Because if I let go of her hand she will go shopping.

Q. My wife spent two hours at the Beauty Shop and came home with nothing being done. What was she doing there for two hours?
A. I suppose she was just getting an estimate.

Q. I heard that a doctor gave a man six months to live and then in six months he gave him another six months to live. What happened with this?
A. The man didn't pay his bill in the first six months.

Q. Why do football players put black lines under their eyes?
A. The official answer given by football players is that eye black is a grease or strip applied under the eyes to reduce glare. However, no study has conclusively proven this. It is a form of functional makeup. Our own study has determined that the players actually think it looks cool. Players who don't wear this makeup are often considered pussies thus everyone wears it because it looks cool. The butterfly tattoo on a certain quarterback's ass looks cool too.

Q. How much sanitizer should I use each time I enter a new environment?
A. We've seen your hands, we suggest three large pumps.

Q. Is there such a thing as a quick question?
A. No. But there is such a thing as a quick answer.

Q. What would happen if all of the bumpy roads suddenly all became very smooth roads?
A. All of the travel stories would suddenly become boring.

Q. A child asked his grandfather this question: "Papa, what do you remember to be the best part of your childhood?"
A. We had lots of fun playing outside in all seasons, building things from scraps, exploring all of the neighborhoods, meeting new friends and we played cards and tried to do magic tricks. Then social media took over.

Q. What was the theme of President Biden's inaugural address?
A. We aren't sure about that, but we are sure that Garth Brooks had new hair plugs when he sang "Amazing Grace" at the inauguration.

Q. Some people have magnets of religious icons on their refrigerators. If God had a refrigerator what magnet would he have?
A. A picture of Chuck Norris.

Q. I have a house, a car, a job and make good money. My immature video game playing son hits me up for money all the time. So, when he scored an 88 on his biology exam, I also took it to teach him a lesson. I got a score of 61. What does that mean?
A. You need to turn over your car, house and money to him since he can obviously invest it wiser than you. You better keep your job though, in case your son needs a bigger bankroll.

Q. My wife thinks I should stop yelling at my son. How do I convince her that yelling at him is necessary?
A. Tell her it is a technique used by experts to motivate selective listeners.

Q. Do you know why I talk to myself?
A. Sometimes you need expert advice.

Q. I've heard that football players last season saw a rise in concussions. What was the cause of that?
A. It appears to be head butting each other after a touchdown.

Q. I was wondering if yoga would be good for exercise. Is it?
A. You won't even bend over to pick up a coin on the floor so I don't think you will like yoga

Q. Why can't teenagers manage their time?
A. Research has shown that they have the management skills of a carrot.

Q. I am tired of exercising to get rid of my excess weight. How can I look slimmer without all of the exercise stuff?
A. We recommend you try to learn photo-shop and work on your photos.

Q. I lost a contact lens. What should I do?
A. Announce to everyone nearby that you lost your contact lens and a lot of people will help you find it. Haven't you noticed; people love to look for them.

Q. I am afraid of germs. Is there anything I can do to break my fear of germs?
A. Of course. Use a porta-podi until you no longer fear the germs.

Q. When will I know that I have enough money to retire?
A. When you no longer complain about the cost of airport food.

Q. I see eating six large mozzarella cheese sticks as disgusting. What do you think?
A. If you are eating them to stop diarrhea, that is fine. But eating six mozzarella breadsticks as an appetizer for $8, now that is disgusting.

Q. Have you ever heard the phrase "If you love something, you must set it free?"
A. Sure, I follow that advise whenever I come across a distressed pie.

Q. What do you think about kids nowadays watching cartoons like Sponge Bob Square Pants?
A. We think they will become sissies and snowflakes. They need to see some real powerful cartoons like Yosemite Sam and Foghorn Leghorn. Those guys were real problem solvers.

Q. I want to be important even after I die. Where is that possible?
A. Chicago, you can still vote there after you die.

Q. As I get older my eye sight seems to be getting poorer. Is there any advantage to having poor eye sight?
A. Some people have found that older age and poor eye sight allows them to see through some people.

Q. What are the three symptoms of laziness?
A. Going to bed early, sleeping in every morning and taking long naps.

Q. Do we all have that one friend that we greet with a swear word insult?
A. No, just you.

Q. What is the opposite of irony?
A. For you it is wrinkly.

Q. Why is there a handle inside the car above the passenger front seat?
A. That is for your use when you teach a teenager how to drive.

Q. Have you ever heard the term "getting too big for your britches?"
A. Yes, when you were little it meant that you were getting into trouble, now it means that you are getting fat.

Q. What is one of the strongest scientific theories in the world?
A. For every male action there is a stronger female reaction.

Q. What happened to the man that went before the judge for drinking too much?
A. When the judge told him he was there for drinking he said, "ok, then, let's get stated."

Q. Why do Jewish mothers make great parole officers?
A. They never let anyone finish their sentences.

Q. Why do so many women order Won Ton at a Chinese restaurant?
A. Because Won Ton spelled backwards is Not Now.

Q. What is the best advice to give to a young bride?
A. Never underestimate the number of times your husband will do things wrong.

Q. What is the secret to keeping friends?
A. Never tell anyone that you had a good night's sleep.

Is This True? Or Are You Being a Wise Guy?

Q. Now that Biden is president, have we ever heard who won the Democratic caucus in Iowa?
A. No, but we know it wasn't Joe. However, we will know the winner some day since Iowa can't have another caucus until they complete the tabulation of the previous one.

Q. What happened to the politicians promise to end kids going to bed hungry?
A. They spent $100 million getting elected instead.

Q. Could you list everything that people don't argue about on Facebook?
A. Sure, here it is: (crickets)

Q. I just got a subscription to Ancestry.com. I bet you $5000 that you can't guess what I just discovered about my ancestry.
A. We'll take that bet. After some discussion, the staff has figured that you have traced your ancestry back 62 generations and discovered that your ancestor was a prostitute in ancient Rome and may have had an affair with Julius Caesar. This would explain your receding hair line, the way you walk with a slight limp, your hunched shoulders, club foot, the six fingers on your left hand and the disfigurement of your face before your accident. Were we right?

Q. How did you know that and will you take a check?
A. Lucky guess and no, cash or gold only.

Q. Why do I forget things?
A. Because your brain doesn't want you to remember. Your brain is the smart part of yourself so if it doesn't want you to find your car keys, I'm sure it has a good reason, like it is afraid to ride in the car with you.

Q. What is a score?

A. You may think that it is the results of last night's game. Your team lost 108 to 4. But a score is also an amount. Just like eggs are counted by the dozen, that is 12. Your whiskey consumption is counted by the score, that is 20.

Q. Do you know what a piffle is?

A. First you must say it four times out loud very fast. I'll wait...
Now don't you feel better? You just did a piffle, that is you just did trivial nonsense.

CHAPTER 6

Stories in Minnesota often revolve around the Norwegian immigrant couple, Ole and Lena. Much has been written about this couple but we offer here a sample of Minnesota humor as well as discovering some more truth. Just as we don't judge a book by its cover, we don't judge immigrants from looking at Ole and Lena. This is just pure Minnesota.

Direct from Minnesota

The toilet seat was invented by a Norwegian in Minnesota. Twenty years later a North Dakotan improved it by putting a hole in the middle.

OUTHOUSE PROBLEM

When Ole accidentally lost 50 cents in the outhouse, he immediately threw in his watch and billfold. He explained, 'I'm not going down dere yust for 50 cents!'

VE COULDN'T AFFORD MORE

Two Norwegians from Minnesota went fishing in Canada and returned with one fish. 'The way I figger it, dat fish cost us $400' said the first fellow. 'Vell,' said the other, 'At dat price it's a good ting ve only caught one!'

THE RELATIONS

Ole and Lena were getting on in years. Ole was 92 and Lena was 89. One evening they were sitting on the porch in their rockers and Ole reached over and patted Lena on her knee. 'Lena, vat ever happened tew our sex relations?'

He asked.

'Vell, Ole, I yust don't know,' replied Lena.

'I don't tink ve even got a card from dem last Christmas'

MUSIC SOLUTION

Ole bought Lena a piano for her birthday. A few weeks later, Lars inquired how she was doing with-it.

'Oh,' said Ole, 'I persvaded her to switch to a clarinet.'

'How come?' asked Lars.

'Vell,' Ole answered, 'because vith a clarinet, she can't sing.'

THE PRANK CALL

The phone rings in the middle of the night when Ole and Lena are in bed and Ole answers.

'Vell how da hell should I know, dats two tousand miles from here' he says and hangs up.

'Who vas dat?' asks Lena. 'I donno, some fool vanting to know if da coast vas clear.'

HONEYMOON TRIP

On their honeymoon trip, they were nearing Minneapolis when Ole put his hand on Lena's knee.

Giggling, Lena said, 'Ole, you can go farther dan dat if you vant to'. So Ole drove to Duluth.

DA PARTY

Ole was arrested one night while walking bare naked down the streets of the little town of

Alexandria, Minnesota. The policeman, who was a good friend of Ole's said,'Ole..What in the world are you doing? Where are your clothes?

You're naked.'

'Yah, I know,' said Ole. 'You see, I vas over to dat 'playboy' Swen's for his birthday party. Dere vas about ten of us. Der vas boys and girls.'

'Is that right?', his policeman friend asked.

'Yah, Yah, anyvay, dat Swen, he says, 'Everybody get into the bedroom!'

'So vee all go into the bedroom.... where den he yells, 'Everybody git naked!'

'Vel, vee all got undressed. Den he yells, 'Everybody go to town!'

I guess I'm the first one here!'

We know, truth isn't always pleasant.

CHAPTER 7

ANSWERS TO COVID-19 QUESTIONS

In the year 2020 the world was hit with a very serious pandemic that was named Covid-19. Covid comes from the name of a Coronavirus that was first discovered in late 2019. If you lived through this time you will understand the answers to the covid questions since parts of the government went overboard with solutions that many times were not solutions at all. If you were too young or born after the event just enjoy what we thought of those times. The questions and answers found below were written in 2020 during the crisis.

Some Covid-19 Tips

1. In case you struggle with social distancing accuracy, remember that six feet is the average length of a Walmart receipt.
2. Stay away from anyone who says "Ciao."
3. Stay away from stationary bikes. There has been an increase in road rage from stationary bike users.
4. We will know when the government is really serious when they fire Dr. Fauci and replace him with Chuck Norris.
5. Covid-19 is noticeable if you see anyone dipping French fries in milk shakes. Get them to the ER.

Wise guys on Covid-19

Q. Can you tell me a good way to avoid the coronavirus?
A. Don't listen to Justin Bieber music. It has worked for me.

Q. Everyone is buying up the toilet paper around here. I don't have very much left at my house. What should I do?
A. You need to reduce the number of times you go to the bathroom to poo to make your toilet paper last longer. Eat an eight-ounce block of cheese every day should help.

Q. With COVID-19 out there now, when can I expect to see "normal?"
A. Last time we checked, you can still find normal on your washing machine.

Q. We've had a shortage of toilet paper and bottled water, what will be the next item in short supply?
A. We checked the garbage collected in your neighborhood the past month and figure there will soon be a run on Jack Daniels No. 7 and Captain Morgan rum.

Q. My wife is having a birthday soon. What should I get her that will be inexpensive now but in six months should be worth ten times what is costs today?
A. We suggest getting her a barrel of crude oil. Get a dozen if you have room in your garage.

Q. I have a $50 gift card for J.C. Penny, when will I be able to use it?
A. You may have lost the chance to use it at the store. You might want to put in in a frame and hang it on the wall in your home as a collector's item. You should be able to recoup your $50 in about 72 years.

Q. What is your biggest concern about being quarantined in your home?
A. Trying to decide when it's too late for coffee or too early for alcohol.

Q. I keep hearing people say "in these uncertain times." What do they mean by that?
A. Before the present day we always knew what was going to happen.

Q. If people knew what was going to happen, then did they know the South would lose the Civil War?
A. According to the people who use the term "in these uncertain times" the answer is yes.

Q. How do you like working at home?
A. I didn't work at work so what makes you think I'm working at home.

Q. During the quarantine I got my wife a 1000-piece puzzle to keep her busy. What do you think she got me?
A. A list of nursing homes for you to choose from.

Q. Do you think things will change after the covid-19 thing is over?
A. No, you're still going to jail.

Q. I love the Big-Mac and could eat one every day for ever. Is there anything you could get from eating at McDonald's every day?
A. Yes, a stomachache.

Q. They say that when I have stress, I should go to my happy place. Where is your happy place?
A. That's a no brainer, Dairy Queen.

Q. Are you afraid of murder hornets?
A. If you live along the Mississippi River you have a problem with shadflies not murder hornets. I dare these murder hornets to take on the shadflies.

Q. My bathroom scale says I have gained 15 pounds since I began wearing a facemask in public. How can that be?
A. Sure, blame the facemask for you getting fat. You should wear your facemask in the house every time you enter the kitchen.

Q. What is your biggest fear during the Covid-19 pandemic?
A. That the CDC will outlaw buffets.

Q. My favorite chicken wing place doesn't have home delivery. What can I do?
A. Nothing, because Hooters doesn't deliver for the reason that you want them to deliver.

Q. Why does the quarantine make this year seem so long?
A. Because 2020 is a leap year with 29 days in February, 300 days in March and 5 years in May.

Q. I seem to be eating more and gaining weight during the covid-19 self-quarantine. Do I need to do more exercise?
A. No, you need to wear your mask indoors.

Q. I heard that a child could cure the covid-19 pandemic. Who is this child?
A. He is known to have found solutions to many medical problems in less than thirty minutes. His name is Doogie Howser.

Q. I heard we could have been preparing for Covid-19 as early as 1985. Why didn't we start preparing 35 years ago?
A. Doc and Marty didn't set the flux capacitor in their De Lorean for 2020.

Q. I'm afraid that NFL games will be played without any fans in the stadium. Will it still feel like the games I remember?
A. Yes, the TV people will be dubbing in crowd noise and showing old footage of the fans in the stands. It will be just like the old days.

Q. Is there a way to get the experience of a totalitarian state without the danger of being put in jail?
A. Sure, during the covid-19 quarantine, people from Vermont would slip into New York to see what it was like. They never stayed long since there was nothing to buy and nothing to do.

Q. For years I didn't have time to thoroughly clean my house. Then I was quarantined and still didn't clean my house. Can you help me?
A. Lack of time was not the reason you didn't clean your house, laziness was the reason. The answer is no.

Q. What was the worst thing that ever happened to you?
A. Just last week I got a murder hornet caught in my facemask as I was driving to my favorite sit-down restaurant to get some carry out food. I thought I was going to die.

Q. During the Covid-19 quarantine several businesses have gone under. Can you explain why Spencer's Gifts is not one of them?
A. Sure, they are one of the few stores that sells the things people really want.

Is This True? Or Are You Being a Wise Guy?

Q. They say we live in unprecedented times. What did they call the time period before the unprecedented times?
A. My grandfather remembers as a child that his father called the life he was living as prece- dented times.

Q. During the recent quarantine I started drinking more alcohol to relieve my anxiety about staying home. Is there something else that I could drink with less alcohol and would make me be glad I was staying home?
A. We suggest that you have a daily drink of colonoscopy prep.

Q. What was the best thing about pizza delivery in the "good old days?"
A. Today they leave the pizza on your door step, in the "good old days" if they took longer than 30 minutes to deliver it, it was free.

Q. Do you know someone who should not be notified when the quarantine is over?
A. Just one, you.

Q. What do you hate about the grocery stores rules we have today?
A. The one-way tape in the aisles. The can of beans I need is just 2 steps up the aisle the wrong way. Then the stock boy came running up and wrote me a ticket. I had to pay an extra $5 at the checkout for a fine. I'm never going to eat beans again.

Q. What is one of the biggest changes you have seen about men and women since we started the quarantine?
A. We've noticed that more women are going to therapy but men start podcasts.

Q. Did you notice that kids don't get snow days anymore?
A. Yes, remote learning took care of that. Besides, the kids don't play in the snow anymore.

Q. Do I need to wear a mask when I go outside?
A. According to Dr. Fauci, the answer is no. Then the answer is yes. Then the answer is one mask is not enough.

Q. How many masks should I wear?
A. Every expert has a different answer. So, the best thing to do is wear each type of mask that the experts recommend. That means you should wear about 6 masks.

CHAPTER 8

ANSWERS TO STUPID QUESTIONS

Q. What is the fastest land mammal in the world?
A. Recent studies indicate that it is a toddler who was just asked by his father "what's in your mouth?"

Q. Did you know there is not one canary on the Canary Islands?
A. Yes, it's the same with the Virgin Islands- not one canary there either.

Q. Have you noticed how fast a child can pick up dropped things?
A. Oh yah, now I have to decide if I need it anymore before I spend the effort to pick it up.

Q. Sometimes my eyes hurt after drinking coffee. What is the cause of that?
A. You forgot to take the spoon out of your cup.

Q. I have a hard time remembering what day it is. What advise do you have for me?
A. Arrange your underwear with the day of the week written on them and don't get dressed in the dark.

Q. Is it true that Illinois has a department called the Sandwich Police?
A. Yes, and the way you make sandwiches you better stay out of Sandwich, Illinois.

Q. What should I do if I think someone is following me when I driving to the grocery store?
A. Drive like you are in a James Bond movie. That should get rid of them.

Q. My teenage son asked me to explain taxes. What would be a good way to show him what taxes are like.
A. Take him to Poncheros and make him pay for a burrito. Then you eat 41% of it and tell him he gets the rest.

Q. How do I know when I have enough money to be considered rich?
A. You know you are rich when your dog has a dog.

Q. What does it mean when a woman says "What?"
A. She isn't asking you to repeat what you said, she is giving you a chance to change your response.

Q. Some of my friends say I am immature. I am 55 years old and think I am as mature as anyone else. What do you think?
A. Stop going to your friend's houses at night leaving pink flamingos in their yards.

Q. Some drivers seam to ignore my horn when I want to get their attention. What can I do?
A. Start carrying fireworks in your car. It has worked for me.

Q. I'm looking for something fun to do that is different, inexpensive and will be a load of laughs. What might you suggest I do?

A. Tomorrow take two witnesses with you and dress in a blue shirt and tan pants and go to Best Buy. Ask for the manager and then tell him that you quit.

Q. I don't think I can do that, do you have any other ideas?
A. Sure, dress up in a red polo shirt and Khaki pants and take two friends with you to the nearest State Farm Insurance Agency and turn in your resignation?

Q. How is any of this funny?
A. When you take two friends with you they will tell the rest of us how successful you were quitting a job you don't have. We think that will be funny.

Q. They say we live in unprecedented times. What did they call the time period before the unprecedented times?
A. Captain Scott remembers as a child that his father called the life he was living as precedented times.

Q. What was the best thing about pizza delivery in the "good old days?"
A. Today they leave the pizza on your door step, in the "good old days" if they took longer than 30 minutes to deliver it, it was free.

Q. I hear there is a coin shortage. What is the cause of that?
A. I'm not sure about where you live, but in my area, all of my friends decided to clean up our language and started swear buckets.

Q. I have concerns about the decisions the government makes. Is there anything I can do?
A. You obviously are voting for the wrong people. Have you ever considered sending the government something to guide their decisions? We suggest you send them a new Magic 8 ball.

Q. Where is the best place to get really good fresh produce?
A. Down the block in my neighbor's garden. Really good stuff and cheap too.

Q. What do you consider to be the most important technological innovation?
A. Most people would say the automobile or perhaps the miniaturization of the computer so you can wear it on your wrist like Dick Tracy. But for you it is the gravy boat. You can't live without it.

Q. What is one of the most enjoyable things about sitting around the campfire?
A. Seeing a bunch of 50+ year-olds pretend to have the body of a 28-year-old and have the mind of a 12-year-old.

Q. How can just one person, like myself, save ten trees.
A. Try using the receipts you get from fast-food, big box and drugstores in your fireplace this winter instead of wood. That's about 10 trees per year.

Q. Do you know what you will never hear anyone say at a pizza party?
A. For most people you will never hear anyone say the crust is the best part of the pizza, except for you.

Q. I was in the liquor store the other day and I heard the whistle from the theme of "The Good, the Bad and the Ugly." What was that all about?
A. Nothing to fret about. It came from the beer section where Albert Sailhorst was answering his cell phone call from his beer bookie.

Q. I've heard that cardiovascular exercise will help prolong your life. Is this true?
A. We have consulted the visiting Chinese Doctor at the prestigious University of Pidgeon Ridge Medical School, Dr. Chin Not Wong.

Here is what he has to say about that: "Heart only good for so many beats, and that it. Don't waste on exercise. Everything wear out eventually. Speeding up heart not make you live longer; it like saying extend life of car by driving faster. Want to live longer? Take nap.

Q. Over the years, what has caused you the most pain?
A. The inability of the bed post and my right big toe to get along.

Q. Throughout your lifetime, have you had more accomplishments or stories to tell.
A. My biggest accomplishment has been to tell many true stories, most are sad but funny because I'm not very intelligent.

Q. Do you have any ideas how to keep burglars away from my house?
A. If you have kids in college, post the tuition bills on your front door.

Q. I saw a car with an elderly couple drive by with a sign in the window that said "just married." I think that was rather bold for elderly newlyweds. What do you think?
A. That couple has been married for 40 years, thus the sign of lost bliss.

Q. How do I keep my kids from running out to the ice cream truck when it comes down my street?
A. Tell them that when the music is playing, they are out of ice cream.

Q. What is a newborn baby?
A. A redundant statement.

Q. What does a rodeo teach people about life?
A. That some people do stupid things with wild animals. Which of the things you see at a rodeo would you like to do? How about at a bull fight? If you chose an answer, I rest my case.

Q. In this digital age I think it is a good idea for students to learn how to write in cursive. Is there anything else that you think they should learn that is being forgotten?
A. Yes, how to use a rotary phone and how to read the hands on a clock. It also wouldn't hurt them to put away their video games and play a game of pong.

Q. Is there anything that still fits you that you haven't worn in ten years?
A. Only my hat.

Q. What would make a politician more interesting to watch?
A. If liars pants really did catch on fire.

Q. What is the cause of wind?
A. Recent research has determined that wind can be generated by eating a large helping of beans and cooked cabbage and wash it down with beer. Then wait 30 minutes or jump up and down for 10 minutes. There may be some rumbling before you hear the wind break.

Q. What comes before maybe?
A. April A.

Q. What comes after maybe?
A. If you think June C comes after maybe, boy are you gullible. What comes after maybe depends on what was offered such as a bribe of cash or favors. Then, what comes after maybe is yes.

Q. I don't understand the controversy over Roe v. Wade. Could you explain it to me?
A. It mainly has to do with whether you want to get your pants wet and how deep the water is. Deep water you will row and shallow water you will wade.

Q. Why is it that some people never seem to be embarrassed?
A. Because you can't be embarrassed if you don't care what people think.

Q. If a woman says "I'm not mad at you," what does she really mean?
A. It has the same meaning as the dentist saying "You won't feel a thing."

Q. My teenage son seems to be living in another world. What can I do?
A. Start recording the things that he does that seem alien to you. Here is an example of alien things you may observe: pouring milk into the bowl before the cereal, eating soft butter with a spoon like ice cream, thoroughly covering ice cream with pepper before eating it or refusing to eat at McDonalds because he prefers humus.

Q. I heard that you have been in love with the same woman for 50 years. What is your secret to this long relationship?
A. My wife has never found out about it.

Q. What are the three words a woman never wants to hear when she is making love?
A. Honey, I'm Home.

Q. My wife lost her credit card and I decided not to tell the credit card company. Do you know why?
A. I have a pretty good idea. The thief probably spends less than your wife.

Q. I always see you at the shopping mall holding hands with your wife. That's so sweet. Why do you always do that?
A. Because if I let go of her hand she will go shopping.

Q. My wife spent two hours at the Beauty Shop and came home with nothing being done. What was she doing there for two hours?
A. I suppose she was just getting an estimate.

Q. What was the theme of President Biden's inaugural address?
A. We aren't sure about that, but we are sure that Garth Brooks had new hair plugs when he sang "Amazing Grace" at the inauguration.

Q. What is one of the biggest changes you have seen about men and women since we started the quarantine?
A. We've noticed that more women are going to therapy but men start podcasts.

Q. I heard that a doctor gave a man six months to live and then in six months he gave him another six months to live. What happened with this?
A. The man didn't pay his bill in the first six months.

Q. Why do football players put black lines under their eyes?
A. The official answer given by football players is that eye black is a grease or strip applied under the eyes to reduce glare. However, no study has conclusively proven this. It is a form of functional makeup. Our own study has determined that the players actually think it looks cool. Players who don't wear this makeup are often considered pussies thus everyone wears it because it looks cool. The butterfly tattoo on a certain quarterback's ass looks cool too.

Q. How much sanitizer should I use each time I enter a new environment?
A. We've seen your hands, we suggest three large pumps.

Q. Is there such a thing as a quick question?
A. No. But there is such a thing as a quick answer.

Q. What would happen if all of the bumpy roads suddenly all became very smooth roads?
A. All of the travel stories would suddenly become boring.

Q. A child asked his grandfather this question: "Papa, what do you remember to be the best part of your childhood?"
A. We had lots of fun playing outside in all seasons, building things from scraps, exploring all of the neighborhoods, meeting new friends and we played cards and tried to do magic tricks. Then social media took over.

Q. Did you notice that kids don't get snow days anymore?
A. Yes, remote learning took care of that. Besides, the kids don't play in the snow anymore.

Q. When will I know that I have enough money to retire?
A. When you no longer complain about the cost of airport food.

Q. What is the best advice to give to a young bride?
A. Never underestimate the number of times your husband will do things wrong.

Q. What is the secret to keeping friends?
A. Never tell anyone that you had a good night's sleep.

Q. Now that Biden is president, have we ever heard who won the Democratic caucus in Iowa?
A. No, but we know it wasn't Joe. However, we will know the winner some day since Iowa can't have another caucus until they complete the tabulation of the previous one.

Q. What happened to the politicians promise to end kids going to bed hungry?
A. They spent $100 million getting elected instead.

Q. Could you list everything that people don't argue about on Facebook?
A. Sure, here it is: (crickets)

Q. Should I tell my parents I'm adopted?
A. Don't do it. That would ruin your inheritance.

Q. If I eat myself will I get twice as big or disappear completely?
A. This is new territory for the command staff. You will have to set up a date for us to watch you. Then we will know the true answer.

Q. Does it take 18 months for twins to be born?
A. That's right, nine months each. And if your mother delivers quintuplets, she will be pregnant for eight years.

Q. Hey wise guys, help me understand why the CDC said that people who are fully vaccinated for covid-19 now must wear a face mask both indoors and outdoors. Aren't fully vaccinated people safe from the virus without wearing a mask?
A. The CDC has changed its position several times. They have now developed a new plan that will not ever change, it is called the extra precaution plan. The CDC is reviewing all health issues and will make new protocols in every area. Expect the new seatbelt protocol to require wearing seatbelts even when out of your car.

Q. How can I wear a seatbelt when not in my car?
A. A new company in Dover, Delaware now makes the out of car seatbelt. We have no further information at this time although

we have contacted the company and are awaiting a reply from the company CEO Hunter Biden.

Q. Do you think NASA invented thunderstorms to cover up the sound of space battles?
A. It's not the question that we are concerned about, but why you might think this is true. Before NASA existed, it was believed that the gods were doing battle. That is still the answer and NASA is lying.

Q. I swallowed an ice cube whole, and I haven't pooped it out. Need I be concerned?
A. Be sure to wait at least three days. If it still hasn't come out, drink a gallon of hot water. That will dislodge it.

Q. How big is the specific ocean?
A. Really big. You can't even see across it to the other side.

Q. How am I sure I'm the real mom of my kid?
A. Just look at him; big nose, droopy eyes, ugly complexion and all those warts. It's yours.

Q. Is there a pill that'll make me gay?
A. Don't worry about it, we slipped it into your coffee last year.

Q. How do I ask a question on Yahoo Answers? (This was asked on Yahoo! Answers.)
A. There are two ways to do this. The slow way is to send it to google questions. The faster way is to ask Captain Scott.

Q. Why are the holes in cat's fur always in the right places for their eyes?
A. It's just pure luck. Some cats have to have the hair shaved around their eyes or they keep bumping into things.

Q. What does a quarter till 4 mean? like, why is it called that?! cause a quarter is worth 25 cents, so why is it 15 min?!
A. It's true that a quarter is worth 25 cents but with inflation the way it is, it is only worth 15 minutes on a clock.

Q. Are chickens considered animals or birds?
A. They can be considered for breakfast, lunch or dinner.

Q. Is it possible for tattoos to get passed on genetically from parent to child?
A. Yes of course. That's why there are many sailing ship tattoos but not very many aircraft carriers. You should probably have that butterfly tattoo on your ass removed, it was alright on your grandmother.

Q. If I shave my golden retriever like a lion, will the other dogs respect him more?
A. Yes, of course. You should do that right away to improve your dog's self-esteem.

Q. Can your baby get pregnant if you have sex while pregnant?
A. That's why you should never have sex during pregnancy. You and your wife should switch to vegetables like everyone else during pregnancy.

Q. Where do lost socks go when they go missing?
A. Where do your pants go when they go missing? That's where the socks went.

Q. What happens to the people born on Feb. 29? Do they stay one until 4 years pass?
A. Your question assumes that something happens to people born on Feb. 29. If you know what happens to people born on your birthday

then you know the answer. The second part of your question asks if they stay one for four years? Did you? If you did, so did they.

Q. Does looking at a picture of the sun hurt your eyes?
A. Nope. Everyone on the staff tried it. It must be just you.

Q. I lost my child in Home Depot. Where should I go to look for him?
A. If that is the kid that called an elderly gentleman an "old fart" go check the red LG in the dryer section.

Q. What do you know about me that I have never told anyone?
A. Based on some of the questions that you have asked the wise guys, we know that your fourth favorite color is aqua.

Q. How do I know if someone is using my Netflix account?
A. Change the password and see who calls you.

Q. What if I don't want to be a good example for other people?
A. Then at least be a good warning on what not to be.

Q. Should I be concerned about people wanting social justice?
A. Yes, because people wanting social justice are disguising their real intention and that is that they really want revenge.

Q. I'm concerned that in this woke world others will feel offended about the things I might say or do. What should I do?
A. Nothing. Just because someone is offended does not mean they are right.

Q. What was the biggest disappointment you had this week?
A. I decided to unfriend you on Facebook only to find out that you beat me to it.

Q. There are a lot of new sports added to the Olympics this year. Are there any other sports you think that would attract more athletes as well as spectators?
A. Only one comes to mind: belly flops.

Q. Why do sharks attack people at the beach?
A. You would be angry too if a bunch of guys in speedos showed up at your house.

Q. I have a problem when the doctor tells me to drink eight glasses of water each day. What should I do?
A. You didn't seem to have a problem with eight glasses of beer last night. See if the doctor will approve of substituting beer for water. It has water in it.

Q. At what age does a boy's period start?
A. The same as a girl's period. At the end of the first sentence.

Q. Why doesn't the Earth fall down?
A. It can't fall down, but the sky can. Just ask Chicken Little.

Q. If Batman's parents are dead, then how was he born?
A. The same way all children are born. Do we need to draw you a picture?

Q. Yes, will you draw me a picture?
A. No, you pervert.

Q. I keep hearing the saying, "Let's go Brandon." What does that mean?
A. It is not a cheer for NASCAR driver Brandon Johnson. President Bidden is Brandon. It is actually a derogatory statement criticizing every bad thing that Biden has done. "Let's go" also could mean F U.

Q. What is a grawlix?
A. This is a grawlix: &%#@$. When it is used in a sentence the grawlix is a substitute for your favorite cuss word. "Let's Go Brandon" is technically a grawlix.

Q. What does F U mean?
A. It means &%#@$ You.

Q. Why is it called 'shipping' if it goes by truck?
A. Years ago, all packages were sent on ships. Today many packages are now sent by the trucking industry. We suggest you stop shipping packages and instead have them trucked.

Q. How do bankruptcy attorneys make any money?
A. Just like all of the other attorneys, they gouge you for their services.

Q. If animals could talk, which would be the rudest?
A. It is already you. The human animal. The others don't stand a chance.

Q. Is cereal soup?
A. Only after you pour on the milk. Before that it is considered candy.

Q. How many chickens would it take to kill an elephant?
A. Just the last one. The other 115,000 chickens are accessories to the fact.

Q. What does it mean when a restaurant advertises new menu items?
A. It means they just raised the prices on everything.

Q. When I tell a joke and the person not laughing says, "you're funny," what does that mean?
A. It means you are not funny.

Q. What do you think about a person that eats ribs with a knife and fork?
A. This person cannot be trusted. It also applies to eating fried chicken.

Q. What sport would be the funniest to add a mandatory amount of alcohol to?
A. Gymnastics comes to mind. A bunch of people jumping and twirling on the rings is just like the drunks at the campfire. Probably will be more puking.

Q. Would you rather have no nose, or no arms?
A. I would rather have my nose and arms and watch you picking up things without arms.

Q. What is your spirit animal?
A. Mine is the fox, able to sneak around the chicken house. Yours is the jack-ass and I think you know why.

Q. Which sport do you think they'll invent next?
A. Probably roller bowling. On a rink the size of a hockey rink, ten players on each side try to knock down pins or skaters. Any skater who falls down is out of the game. Once a team is out of players the score is tallied like bowling plus 10 points per player knocked over.

Q. Do you think cavemen had nightmares about cavewomen?
A. Sure, because I know you still do.

Q. What's the most useless word?
A. Using the word like to describe something. Example, I ate a sandwich like it was good, like I would eat it again, like you know, I liked it. So, what kind of sandwich was it?

Q. What sound would be the scariest if you could hear it?
A. The screaming of the Banshee when she is coming for you.

Q. What is the coolest sound?
A. The sound of rippling water is soothing unlike that awful snoring you make.

Q. What would you rather have; an arm that regenerates every month, or legs that grows back in every month?
A. Give it a rest. Who told you to send in this question? Toland?

Q. What is the most useful invention of all time?
A. I know you think it is the gravy boat but give some thought to electrical generating. If you think of something that requires electricity, then we rest our case.

Q. What is your favorite holiday?
A. Nothing can beat Festivus.

Q. What do you do in your spare time?
A. Recently I spent some time answering these stupid questions. Only thing worse than this was you writing them.

Q. Which smells better, fresh cut grass or bread baking in the oven?
A. Here is a test to determine the answer. Someone will drive you blindfolded to a hog farm where you will smell fresh bread and grass clippings and tell the driver the answer.

Q. What would be your dream job?
A. Getting a paycheck from the Publishers Clearing House sounds good, But, you actually have to work at a job. You look like you should unclog drains at the sewage treatment plant.

Q. If you could be any type of plant or animal, what would you be?
A. We suspect that you would want to be a stinkweed or a skunk.

Q. What would be the hardest thing to give up?
A. You don't want to give up having a bowel movement.

Q. What word is spelled incorrectly in every single dictionary?
A. The word is Incorrectly.

Q. What goes up and down but can't move?
A. We thought it was you that time you got stuck in that pickle barrel, but on second thought it's a staircase.

Q. What goes up but never down?
A. We bet that you are so smart that you wouldn't say it was your age.

Q. What will you give up, brushing your teeth or wiping your butt.
A. What a choice; you either get rotten teeth and bad breath or an unending desire to scratch your ass. Swamp ass is so miserable, I'll give up brushing my teeth and start chewing gum.

Q. Crime doesn't pay… does that mean my job is a crime?
A. Yes, because your job performance is so bad no one will pay you.

Q. Do fish ever get thirsty?
A. Only when you pull them out of the water. They tend to then get dry mouth and begin to smell a little fishy.

Q. Do hummingbirds hum because they don't know the words?
A. Of course, they can't talk so they can't sing.

Q. Do pilots take crash-courses?
A. Yes they do. When this is about to happen, the pilot will put on his parachute and jump out the pilot's door. If you see a parachute go past your window on your next flight then you will know that a crash is imminent.

Q. Do you think that when they asked George Washington for ID that he just whipped out a coin?
A. It seems that you think Washington was on the quarter when he was still alive. But then we are assuming that you meant a quarter but you might have meant a penny. Actually, we should be discussing if coins are an acceptable form of ID. Glue some picture of yourself onto a quarter and use that for an ID next time you buy some beer. Let's see how that turns out for you.

Q. Why doesn't glue stick to the inside of the bottle?
A. It does. Leave the lid off of the glue bottle and let the glue dry. It might take a few days. If it's Elmer's glue, it dries clear, so put a photo in the glue to create a nice picture inside of a blob.

Q. Does a man-eating shark eat women, too?
A. You are such a sexist. Sharks aren't and will even eat you.

Q. How can you tell when it is time to tune your bagpipes?
A. Obviously you don't understand musical instruments. You tune the bagpipes when they sound out of tune. We're guessing.

Q. How do you know if honesty is the best policy unless you've tried some of the others?
A. So true. Did you notice we lied in the answer to one of the last six questions? Or maybe we didn't and we are lying now.

Q. How do you write zero in Roman numerals?

A. There is no zero in Roman numerals because the Romans believed that no numeral could represent nothing, the value of zero. However, the Romans could write zero in the Latin alphabet as follows: ZERO.

Q. If you have a cold hot pocket, is it just a pocket?

A. No, it is still a hot pocket because that is the name of it.

Q. Why is it said that an alarm clock is going off when really, it's coming on?

A. Your logic is perfect. Don't confuse the clock with the alarm function. The clock should always be on and the alarm should always be off. Turn the alarm function on to a set time, like 4:01 am. If you want your alarm clock to go off, pull out the plug from the outlet.

Q. What are imitation rhinestones?

A. Here is how you can make your own imitation rhinestones. Take a lens out of your sunglasses. Then throw it onto the sidewalk and stomp on it with you size 13 FFFF wide shoe. Then put on your sunglasses and examine your imitation rhinestones.

Q. What do batteries run on?

A. A light electrical charge. Here is how to test your battery to check if it has any power in it. Pop it into your mouth. You will now know if it has a charge.

Q. What do chickens think we taste like?

A. Because chickens can't talk we will make a guess. Chickens think you taste like humans.

Q. What do you call a bedroom with no bed in it?
A. Just because you can't afford a bed doesn't mean we change the name of the room to the clothes pile room. It's still the bedroom. Lucky for you.

Q. How come people tell you not to stand in front of an emergency exit, if there was an emergency surely you would not stay standing there?
A. You are not to stand in front of the emergency exit because you are not to be the first person to use the exit in case of an emergency. People who are more important than you are always to go first so you should get out of the way until it is your turn.

Q. In libraries, do they put the bible in the fiction or non-fiction section?
A. There is a special section in the library for religious books. You should have asked earlier so you wouldn't have spent so much time in the fiction and nonfiction sections.

Q. Why are both of Sponge Bob's parents round like sea sponges while he is square?
A. Sponge Bob doesn't look like his parents just like you don't look like your parents. We know they claim you were adopted because they can't explain why you look different from them. We think Sponge Bob had bad genes.

Q. Why do they call it 'chili' if it's hot?
A. It's to trick your brain because your brain doesn't like hot foods.

Q. Why do they call it 'life' insurance?
A. It is actually death insurance, but that isn't correct either. You don't buy insurance for your death but for your life. You don't buy

insurance for your car after it crashes but before it crashes. Thus, you buy the insurance before you die. Looking at your health we suggest you buy a large life insurance policy. We see a big payday for you soon.

Q. Why do they make cars go so fast it's illegal?
A. Nobody wants to buy a car that only goes 55 mph downhill with a 30-mph tailwind. That's why that Mini Cooper you drive goes from 0 to 100 in 3.2 seconds. Why else would you buy that?

Q. Why do we call them restrooms when no one goes there to rest?
A. You are wrong. Many people go to the rest room to rest. We suggest you should stop moving, that is rest, while you pee instead of that pacing you do. Your wet pants make you look sloppy.

Q. Why do we have hot water heaters when hot water doesn't need to be heated?
A. I suppose boiling water doesn't need to be placed on the stove either. Where do you think the hot water came from? The river warmed by the sun? The water heater is called a hot water heater so it is not confused with your beer cooler. I suppose a beer cooler doesn't need to be cooled.

Q. Do they call a fortune teller who can't see a "blind seer"?
A. As redundant as that sounds the answer is yes.

Q. Why do you give your two cents worth when it's only a penny for your thoughts?
A. Because what I am thinking for one cent will be worth double when I let you have it.

Is This True? Or Are You Being a Wise Guy?

Q. Why do we need training bras? What can we teach them?

A. I won't tell you what we can teach them. When you grow up you will know.

Q. Why do your feet smell and your nose runs?

A. Your feet smell because they stink and your nose runs because you are sick.

Q. How did Walt Disney figure out how to make people pay to stand in lines all day and then come back for more the next day?

A. People do that for a thrill. Come to my house tonight at 8 pm and I'll give you a thrill for free and no lines.

Q. Why do sleeping pills have warning labels that state: Caution - May Cause Drowsiness?

A. Because that is what they do. Would you take them it they said 'Caution, may cause diarrhea?

Q. What happened to Old Zealand?

A. Everyone left Old Zealand and moved to New Zealand. Now no one remembers where Old Zealand is. Do you?

Q. Which is the other side of the street?

A. Stand where you are and don't move. Now look at the street. Can you see the other side? Now you know where the other side of the street is and strangely that's where you live.

Q. Who opened that first 'oyster' and said "My, my, my. Now doesn't 'this' look yummy!"

A. We couldn't find anyone in history who ever said that and for obvious reasons. Then we realized that you said that and for obvious reasons.

Q. Why are cigarettes sold in gas stations when smoking is prohibited there?
A. That is so people can't sample them before they buy them. Take them off the premises and there is no refund.

Q. Why are highways built so close to the ground?
A. Some highways are built under ground in tunnels. Some are built above ground on pillars called viaducts. Those built on the ground are the cheapest to make. The answer is purely economics.

Q. Why are there flotation devices under plane seats instead of parachutes?
A. That is to prevent people from jumping out of the plane before landing or crashing. Would you jump out of a plane holding on to a rubber inner tube? I didn't think so.

Q. Why are they called "stands" when they're made for sitting?
A. They are made for sitting when there is no action on the field. But once the game begins everyone will stand to watch the game until halftime when they will sit again.

Q. Why do they call someone "late" if they died early?
A. After someone dies they will always be late for every event they are invited to. So late they don't even show up.

Q. Why are the adjectives 'fast as' and 'slow as' often used in conjunction with hell? Is hell slow or fast?
A. Good observation. Since you will be visiting there soon, perhaps you could send us a report.

Q. Why is chess considered a sport?
A. Apparently you have only observed amateur chess that is sometimes so slow that it would be more fun to watch paint dry. Put a chess

clock in the professional chess match with a three-minute time for each player. Now the game must end in six minutes and the player's minds and arms will be moving so fast that they will break a sweat and hit the showers after the match just like in the WWE.

Q. Why is it that when you are sleeping it's called drool but when you are awake it's called spit?
A. You are fooling yourself. Your spit is just controlled drool. Drool is drool.

Q. Why don't they call mustaches "mouth brows?"
A. You can call them that. Start a new trend and show everyone how intelligent you are.

Q. If a teacher were to teach a younger grade than they were teaching before, would they be "degraded"?
A. No it is demoted. Teachers look for promotions to higher grades just like the students. Unfortunately, some teachers never get out of kindergarten.

Q. How come people tell you to stay a kid for as long as you can. Yet the moment you do anything childish or immature they tell you to grow up.
A. That never happens to any of us. Maybe you should seek professional help.

Q. How do mermaids make babies?
A. We are not going to describe graphic sex of mermaids, you pervert. Use your imagination.

Q. If Fed Ex and UPS were to merge, would they call the resulting company Fed UP?
A. Probably, it makes perfect sense.

Q. Why are elderly people often called "old people" but children are never called "new people"?
A. That's because the new people are the ones that moved into the house next to yours and have been borrowing things out of your garage.

Q. Do one-legged ducks swim in circles?
A. Where did you see these one-legged ducks, next to the one winged ducks? No, they don't fly in circles and neither do the one-legged ducks. They swim where they want to. If they are swimming in circles it's because that is what they want to do. Do one-legged people walk in circles? I hope you get the point.

Q. Why do you get on a bus and a train but get into a car?
A. Because that is what you do. Go ahead get on a car and see if you can hang on while someone drives you to the store.

Q. If marbles are not made of marble, why are they called marbles?
A. Those round glass spheres known as marbles are called that because they make the same noise if you shake a bag of marbles as you do when you shake your head.

Q. Why is it called lipstick if you can still move your lips?
A. Try the lipstick again. You're not putting enough on.

Q. Why is it called tourist season if we can't shoot at them?
A. It is illegal to shoot a tourist without a license. You need to go to the sheriff's office and tell the deputy that you want to shoot tourists. He'll take care of it for you.

Q. What happens if you get a paper cut from a Get-Well card?
A. You will get more get-well cards.

Q. Can you read a picture book?
A. Sure. Apparently, you can't.

Q. Why are dandelions considered weeds when daisies are considered flowers?
A. A connoisseur does not consider dandelions as weeds. Dandelions can be made into a fine wine and you could make some money harvesting those yellow flowers in your yard. Unfortunately, you are not a connoisseur and as far as flowers go, you could be described as a pansy.

Q. Why do people seem to read the Bible a whole lot more as they get older.
A. They're cramming for their final exam.

Q. Why whenever you start to sing, you automatically sing in a higher voice than you talk?
A. That doesn't happen to everyone. If it happens to you, you need to remove your jockey shorts before singing.

Q. If you called the police station to talk to an officer and he is not there, would that be considered a cop out?
A. Yes, you are such a genius.

Q. Can a school teacher give a homeless child homework?
A. Yes, it would be embarrassing to call it cardboard box work.

Q. Why do mattresses have designs on them when they're always covered with sheets?
A. The designs help camouflage those yellow stains.

Q. If a person suffered from amnesia and then was cured would they remember that they forgot?
A. Put yourself in this situation. You don't have amnesia and you can't remember what you forgot. The answer is no.

Q. What hair color do they put on the driver's license of a bald man?
A. If this is your situation, be prepared to tell them the color of your pubic hair.

Q. What happens if you take No-Doze and wash it down with Nyquil?
A. You will probably get sick from this. If you take the antidote at the same time you won't want to sleep. The antidote is a large dose of laxatives.

Q. What happens when you swallow your pride?
A. You will choke on your self-esteem.

Q. What if someone died in the living room?
A. What if they did? It is not an issue but before you call the coroner you should hide the chicken wings.

Q. The label on a package says "Open here". What is the protocol if the package says, "Open somewhere else"?
A. Then open it somewhere else, probably outside.

Q. Where did Webster look up the definitions when he wrote the dictionary?
A. He just made things up like we do here.

Q. Why is it when two planes almost hit each other it is called a "near miss"?
A. That is what happened. They almost hit each other but missed. What do you want to call it, "Chicken?"

Is This True? Or Are You Being a Wise Guy?

Q. Why is it called 'after dark', when it is really after light?

A. Remember, as far as the movement of the sun goes, after dark comes light, and after light comes dark in a continuous cycle. If you come home after dark then it is already light.

Q. Why is it called a TV "set" when you only get one?

A. You get one TV but you should also get two chairs. If you buy a TV set then you get two chairs with that. Be sure to ask the salesman for your chairs the next time you buy a TV set. Some stores are now selling the TV without the set, so if you pay for the set, demand your chairs.

Q. Why is a women's prison called a penal colony?

A. It has something to do you your perverted mind. You can sign up at the local penal colony to be a conjugal volunteer. Probably something you should do as your civic duty.

Q. Why is a person who plays the piano called a pianist, but a person who drives a race car not called a racist?

A. Who said the race car driver isn't a racist? He drives a race car, doesn't he?

Q. Why do you need an appointment to see a psychic?

A. You need an appointment so you know when to go. The psychic already knows you are coming.

Q. Why does a grapefruit look nothing like a grape?

A. Because grapefruit grows on a tree and grapes grow on a vine. They have nothing in common except they both taste the same.

Q. How can there be "self-help GROUPS"?

A. If you are reading all of these questions and answers it is obvious that you need help and if you provided some of the questions it may be too late for you. The groups meet periodically at various campfires to share their intelligence. Good luck and don't be shy.

Q. If you saw a heat wave, would you wave back?
A. No, but I am sure you would.

Q. If you're born again, do you have two bellybuttons?
A. No, bellybuttons are reusable just like your sphincter.

Q. Is a sleeping bull, a bull-dozer?
A. You are very clever, of course it is.

Q. Is a small pig called a hamlet?
A. Yes, and the small pig jowls are very tender and should be eaten with a nice merlot wine sauce with garlic. We know you are tempted to use ketchup but don't do it, it will spoil the atmosphere.

Q. Is an oxymoron a really dumb bovine?
A. Sure, and if you drop the oxy we have you.

Q. What is a refried bean? Why do they have to fry it twice?
A. "Refried" doesn't mean the beans have been fried twice. The word comes from the Spanish name for the dish—frijoles refritos. In Spanish "refritos" means "well fried." But if your beans are English, then you have to fry them twice to get the best flavor.

Q. What is shaved ice? Did it have hair on it before it was shaved?
A. Yes, your logic is perfect to qualify to be a contestant on Jeopardy.

Q. Can atheists get insurance for acts of God?
A. Sure, someone will sell you an insurance policy on anything. I'm still holding a policy of your life insurance. I have a feeling I will get a payoff soon.

Q. What do you call a male ladybird?
A. A gay bird.

Q. What would you use to dilute water?
A. Typically for each gallon of water add a quart of dehydrated H2O.

Q. If you're in hell, get mad at someone, where do you tell them to go?
A. You may not understand this answer so be sure to think long about it. You tell them to go to the devil's pitchfork.

Q. Why do grocery stores buy so many checkout line registers if they only keep 3 or 4 open?
A. Sometimes a register burns out from over use, so you go to the extra registers.

Q. Why do mattresses have springs, if they aren't made for jumping on?
A. You have been misinformed. Who said they weren't for jumping on?

Q. Why do people tell you when they are speechless?
A. They are letting you know that they have nothing to say. What do you want speechless people to do? Just stand there in silence?

Q. Why do the signs that say "Slow Children" have a picture of a running child?
A. You know children will do the opposite of what they are told to do. Be sure to tell your children to run across street so they will do what the sign says.

Q. If the speed of movement is slower than the speed of light - how fast is a moving light?
A. Check the headlights of a moving car. No matter how fast or slow the car moves the light gets out farther than the car every time. There is your proof that light moves faster than movement.

Q. If electricity comes from electrons, does morality come from morons?
A. That's right and you are a fine example, I might add.

Q. If you fed a bee nothing but oranges, would it make marmalade?
A. This is the perfect example that you should not believe everything you read on the internet.

Q. How come thaw and unthaw mean the same thing?
A. They don't. Unthaw means to refreeze the object.

Q. If I melt dry ice, can I take a bath without getting wet?
A. In theory yes, in reality you will want to wear a lot of heavy clothing while bathing in dry ice because it is very cold.

Q. If the product says "Do not use if seal is broken", how are you supposed to open it and use it?
A. You must open it from the other end.

Q. If time heals all wounds, how come bellybuttons don't fill in?
A. Silly you, your bellybutton is not a wound, it is your birth dimple.

Q. If work is so terrific, how come they have to pay you to do it?
A. They don't have to pay you, you can refuse to be paid and just enjoy the terrific job. You will need to pick up some lousy part-time work to pay the bills.

Q. Is a hot car cool or is a cool car hot?
A. Yes to both questions. The terms hot and cool mean the same thing when talking about cars. They mean opposite things when talking about the stew you just made.

Q. Is a man full of wonder a wonderful man?
A. Typically this would be true as there are many fine examples. However, in your case, we can tell by some of your questions that you wonder about some strange things so we reserve the right to call you wonderful. Just look at the next question that you recently sent in.

Q. Is a duck's Hiney waterproof?
A. Really, this is what you wonder about? Have you seen ducks sinking by taking on water through their hiney? How about yourself? Drinking through your hiney, although possible its really only for experienced hiney drinkers. You may need help to practice this and I know a few guys who would be happy to help you.

Q. How can you hear yourself think?
A. Turn off any devise that makes noise, TV, stereo, cell phone, then plug your ears with plenty of cotton. Now think about your next question you will be sending us. See, it works.

Q. How can you chop down a tree and then chop it up?
A. Let's say the tree is 30 feet tall and you chop it down and it falls to the ground. Now you chop it into firewood and neatly stack behind your garage in a pile that is 8 feet tall and 20 feet long. Now it is chopped up.

Q. If Americans throw rice at weddings, do the Chinese throw hamburgers?
A. Have you seen this? Does everyone bring a bag of hamburgers to the wedding? This is so ridiculous that we won't tell you that they really through French fries.

Q. What's the difference between a wise man and a wise guy?
A. Finally an important question. A wise man is very smart and you would be right to follow his advice. A wise guy will give you advice about some stupid question that you should not follow.

Q. What would happen if an Irresistible Force met an Immovable Object?
A. This is the big bang theory. It creates a new world.

Q. Where in the nursery rhyme does it say humpty dumpty is an egg?
A. It doesn't. You are the one who says he is. Maybe he was a Lego figure.

Q. Why do they say "getting my dog fixed" if afterwards it doesn't work anymore?
A. We didn't want the dog to get over rambunkuous so we fixed that. Now he is a lazy dog like his master.

Q. Why do you click on start to exit Microsoft Windows?
A. That is where you will find the exit button. Go ahead, see if you can find it somewhere else.

Q. If there's an exception to every rule, is there an exception to that rule?
A. Yes, this rule is solid and exceptional.

Q. Is a sleeping bag a nap sack?
A. It sure can, if you want to nap there?

Q. Why is the blackboard green?
A. Original blackboards were black, but later green ones were developed but the name didn't change. Now schools have whiteboards. Soon you will see them in other colors but probably never black.

Q. On the periodic table, why do some elements have symbols with letters that aren't even in the word?
A. This has something to do with language. Not all elements come from the English language so if it came from German the German word and symbol is used instead of English.

Q. If you try to fail and succeed, what did you just do?
A. It is true that most people who want to fail have actually succeeded.

Q. Is the opposite of "out of whack" "in whack"?
A. Yes.

Q. Why are toe nail clippers bigger than finger nail clippers when your toe nails are smaller than your finger nails?
A. Just because you have little feet doesn't mean some people won't need those big clippers. Ask someone with a size 15 shoe if you can see his toe nails.

Q. If Practice makes perfect, and nobody's perfect, then why practice?
A. That's why you're not very good at anything. With that attitude, you will never improve. Are you still seeing your barber to fix your teeth?

Q. What's the opposite of opposite?
A. The opposite of opposite is the same. If white is the opposite of black, then white is the same as white.

Q. Can good looking Eskimo girls be called hot?
A. The one's we've seen are. You need to stop looking for Eskimo girls at the fish market.

Q. Why do people never say "it's only a game" when they're winning?
A. As you know, when you are losing you don't want to put too much into that fact. Next time you play checkers bet your car keys that you will win. Then see if it's only a game.

Q. If somebody vanished without a trace, how do people know they are missing?
A. They are missing, so they are gone. Where did they go? You say without a trace; therefore, they must have vanished.

Q. Can you sentence a homeless man to house arrest?
A. Yes, and it's your turn to use your house.

Q. What do people in China call their good plates?
A. The clean plates. What do you call yours, paper chinette?

Q. If you stole a pen from a bank is it a bank robbery?
A. Yes it is. Next time you are in the bank, slip that pen back onto the counter. You're looking at up to 20 years.

Q. Why are Softballs hard?
A. Original softballs were actually softer than they are today. No one could hit the softball very far so they had to make it hard so it could be hit farther. That's our answer and we're sticking to it.

Q. In France do people just ask for toast and get French toast? Do they have to ask for American toast?
A. It's not French toast in France but fried toast in an egg batter. And nobody asks for American toast. I think you know why.

Q. What do you call a female daddy long legs?
A. We'd like to say a mommy long legs but how can you tell the males from the females. The jury is still out on this one.

Q. Why is the word "dictionary" in the dictionary?
A. All words are in the dictionary so we know what they mean. I suppose you don't know what a dictionary is. Just google it and you will know.

Q. Why are they called stairs inside but steps outside?
A. It is a matter of elegance. The stairs are nice and maybe even carpeted. The steps are out in the weather and are either made of boards or concrete. And the way to your upstairs apartment is called the ladder.

Q. If you mated a bull dog and a shiatsu, would it be called a bullshit?
A. Your logic is so obtuse that we will say yes. We won't waste time with semantics.

Q. How fast do hotcakes sell?
A. That depends on the price and the quality. Really good hotcakes at 25 cents each sell fast as "hotcakes." But your hotcakes made in fatback grease without water at $2 each aren't worth looking at.

Q. How do they get those boats in those glass bottles?
A. Steady hands and long tweezers are necessary and don't glob the glue on the small parts.

Q. What is the name of the phobia for the fear of long words.
A. Hippopotomonstrosesquippedaliophobia?

Q. Why is it that we have the weight of the world on our shoulders but we have to get it off our chests?
A. You have that right. Keep the weight on your shoulders and get things off of your chest. This is how you carry your burdens without hurting yourself. Just don't lose your footing or the burdens will crush you.

Q. If you decide that you're indecisive, which one are you?
A. You are uncertain.

Q. If an anarchist group attained political power, would they by principle have to dissolve their own government?
A. Absolutely, and you better guard your stuff because they think it is now there's.

Q. If Luke took a bath, would the water be lukewarm?
A. Only after he peed in it.

Q. Why do they call the angel of death an angel if all it does is bring pain and suffering?
A. Oh you of little faith; Lucifer is a fallen angel and so is the angel of death. You might want to have a confidential conference with a priest.

Q. Can blind people be dyslexic when they read Braille?
A. Our studies have determined that this can happen when a right handed blind person reads braille with their left hand.

Q. Why do we say "bye bye" but not "hi hi"?
A. "Bye bye" is how we said good bye to babies and small children. If you are still doing this with adults you probably should stop that. We cannot find anyone who ever said "hi hi" except you. You should probably stop that too.

Q. Why do we feel blue?
A. This means that you feel sad. We call it blue because that color is soothing and somewhat melancholy.

Q. What color does a smurf feel when he is down?
A. Tan.

Q. If the universe is expanding, what is it expanding into?
A. Space. It is like knowledge moving into your brain. It displaces space. Space is an invisible nothing.

Q. If you were on a plane going the speed of sound and walked from the back of the plane to the front, would you be walking faster than the speed of sound?
A. Yes, but only a couple feet per second more. We don't recommend jumping up off the plane floor at that speed. Could be painful.

Q. Why are things typed up but written down?
A. When you type, or use your computer, the words are placed above (or up from) the keyboard. When you write by hand you place the paper down (or on a table) to write your message. If you can reverse this trend, you can start a new trend and people will call you a genius. I wouldn't put much hope into this happening.

Q. Why do old men have hair in their ears?
A. Everyone has hair in their ears. Most people have small, thin and light-colored hair that is difficult to see without getting up close. Some men have darker hair and as they age it becomes a bit coarser and easier to see. We recommend you test this idea with a magnifying glass. In a large gathering come up behind people and use your magnifying glass to look into people's ears. We will wait for your report.

Q. If it is a 50 mph per hour wind and you drive your car at 50mph downwind, if you stick your head outside would you feel the wind?
A. According to your logic, no. Now toss a balloon out the window and watch it move next to your car. It looks like it isn't moving but it is actually moving 50 mph. You are so smart.

Q. If water spins clockwise when it drains in the northern hemisphere and water spins counterclockwise when it drains in the southern hemisphere...which way does it spin at the equator?
A. There is no spin, the water just flushes strait down but it has to be exactly on the equator or there will be spin.

Q. Have you ever thought what life would be like if your name was Anonymous? Can you get credit for everything nobody wanted credit for?
A. Nope, we don't know anyone who ever thought about being named anonymous except you. As far as credit goes, you can go for it. Good luck.

Q. Do Siamese twins pay for one ticket or two tickets when they go to movies and concerts?
A. The ticket you buy is for a seat. If you sit in two seats, you need two tickets. If you take five friends to the movies you will only need to buy one ticket if you all sit on each other's lap.

Q. Why did Superman wear his briefs on the outside of his tights?
A. To prevent getting brown stains on his briefs.

Q. Do sheep get static cling when they rub against one another?
A. Of course, that is why they literally stick together in a herd.

Q. Is an alcoholic a drunk that's scared of a hangover?
A. Of course not. An alcoholic is someone who just likes to drink.

Q. Can anybody who has a job go in the "employees only" doors at restaurants?
A. This is the kind of wisdom that makes some people stand out in a crowd. After you go through the "employees only" door stop at the

sink and wash a few dishes, then tell the bus boy that you are going home and want to know where the tip jar is. This could make a pretty good story. Be sure to tell us how this worked out.

Q. Why are you IN a movie, but you are ON TV?
A. If you appear IN the movie you actually were at the film making several months ago, but the TV has to be turned ON to watch anything including the movie you are IN.

Q. If the weather man says "it's a 50% chance of rain" does that mean he has no idea if it's going to rain or not?
A. Yes.

Q. Why do they call him a Skipper when he just stands there?
A. It doesn't matter if he is standing, sitting or skipping; he is still the skipper. If you don't think so, just tell him you don't think he is the skipper and see what happens. I hope you can swim.

Q. If dessert before dinner ruins your appetite for dinner won't eating dinner before dessert ruin your appetite for dessert?
A. This is what the wise guys have been saying for years. Remember, life is uncertain, eat your dessert first.

Q. What do you mean when you say "Life is uncertain, eat your dessert first?"
A. Eat the pie before the chicken. If you choke on a chicken bone someone else will get your pie.

Q. When lightning strikes the ocean why don't all the fish die?
A. That would have to be very strong lightning to kill all of the fish. Certainly a few nearby fish will be zapped.

Q. Why is it when we ask for the check in a restaurant they bring us a bill?
A. Good point, I think you are on to something.

Q. Do people with big eyes see at a wider range than people with smaller eyes?
A. You appeared to be wise in the previous question and now this question is short on vision. Actually, people with big eyes see everything bigger than people with small eyes.

Q. What happens when you say "hi" to your friend on an airplane whose name is Jack?
A. You will get jumped by a bunch of sky marshals. We suggest you say "Hello, Jack."

Q. Why are women and men's shoe sizes different?
A. Because their feet are different sizes.

Q. Why isn't the word 'gullible' in the dictionary?
A. It is in the dictionary and the definition describes you very well. Here is the definition: To be gullible is a failure of social intelligence in which a person is easily tricked or manipulated into an ill-advised course of action.

Q. Why are there pictures of the sun wearing sunglasses when the purpose of sunglasses is to protect your eyes from the sun?
A. If the sun had eyes it would definitely need the sunglasses.

Q. Does it really count in court when an atheist is sworn in under oath using a Bible?
A. The Bible is only used for Christians and Jews because if they lie under oath God will punish them. Atheists just swear an oath that

they promise not to lie. We guess that they think God can't punish them if they don't believe in God. We suspect they may already be punished and if they lie there will be more punishment.

Q. How do they get the air inside the bubble wrap?
A. The air isn't under pressure. When the bubble wrap is manufactured they just capture air as each bubble is sealed. You, on the other hand, pop the bubble by forcing the air out of the bubble by squeezing the bubble. This obviously gives you much amusement.

Q. Can crop circles be square?
A. No circles cannot be squares. You may need a little remedial geometry refresher.

Q. Can you blow a balloon up under water?
A. Yes, but if you are doing this with your mouth you probably need to come up for air each time you blow into the balloon.

Q. Why is it that when we are humming and then we plug our nose, our humming stops? Do people really hum through their nose, or their mouths?
A. The interesting thing is that everyone who just read the question hummed and plugged their nose. More interesting is that the humming did stop, but you can start humming again with your mouth open. You need air to hum and more exactly you need to exhale air to hum. Now try humming while inhaling.

Q. Why would Dodge make a car called Ram?
A. That is the car we all wish we had some times particularly when following a slow driver. Now we can actually own one.

Q. What do vegetarians feed their dogs?
A. Our first guess is dog food. If you are thinking their dogs should eat radishes, cucumbers and asparagus try it out on your dog and tell us how that turned out. Probably should run that through the blender.

Q. If the day before a holiday is called Christmas Eve, is the day after Christmas Adam?
A. No, Adam came before Eve. Therefore, using your logic, Christmas Adam is the day before Christmas Eve.

Q. Do stuttering people stutter when they're thinking to themselves and does it take just as long?
A. Of course, unless they are a speed thinker. Can you speed think?

Q. Why do dogs walk around in circles before lying down?
A. They are just making sure no other dog is about to sneak up behind them and grab their spot. Probably something you should do before you lay down.

Q. Why do most people put more effort into their wedding than their actual marriage?
A. Because it is the last thing the parents are going to pay for, so gouge the hell out of them because you can't afford the stuff you want after the wedding.

Q. Why is it that on the back of a medicine bottle it says "adult" is 12 and above, but the adult age in reality is 18?
A. We are talking drugs here. It is ok to take adult drugs but not adult liquor. Go figure.

Q. If there is a rule that states "i" before "e" except after "c", wouldn't "science" be spelled wrong?
A. Yes, but don't forget there are exceptions to every rule and this is one of them.

Q. Who makes up these spelling rules and who can break them?
A. Somebody told your English teachers and they told you. That's where the rules come from. Everyone can break the spelling rules except when you are spelling things for your English teacher.

Q. If a mirror reverses right and left, why doesn't it reverse up and down?
A. It will if you turn the mirror on its side.

Q. If all the nations in the world are in debt, where did all the money go?
A. For cars, boats, houses and many useless items. For you it went for gum, candy and a paddle ball game.

Q. Did you just turn a mirror on its side?
A. You really should read more nonfiction.

Q. Why is it considered necessary to nail down the lid of a coffin?
A. Just in case the pall bearers drop the coffin, you don't want the body to fall out onto the floor.

Q. Why is it that only adults have difficulty with childproof bottles?
A. No, children have difficulty too.

Q. Why isn't there a special name for the tops of your feet?
A. There is, it's called the dorsal. The bottom of your feet is the plantar surface.

Q. Why do people say PIN number when that truly means Personal Identification Number?
A. You answered your own question. Dah!

Q. Why do people call it an ATM machine, but they know it's really saying Automated Teller Machine?
A. Really, you did it again. And you send these questions to the wise guys because you don't know this.

Q. Why get even, when you can get odd?
A. It's just a 50/50 choice. You probably prefer to get odd.

Q. Why is a carrot more orange than an orange?
A. Are you looking at them in the store? Those are all cleaned up and polished to make them look better. It also means that they cost more. To save money we suggest raiding your neighbor's garden or fruit trees. If you want fruit and vegetables to look nice, then buy them at the store.

Q. Why is it when we laugh in school the teachers say do you find something funny? When obviously we do?
A. Your teacher is making sure you are not laughing at him. Next time, instead of laughing, slip him a note that his zipper is down.

Q. Don't accept candy from strangers, yet on Halloween, its encouraged! Why is that?
A. In the first place the stranger may be a kidnapper. On Halloween, the kidnappers lay low because there are so many kids out that could be a witness.

Q. Just what was the "Baby On Board" sign for? Did it help us decide which car not to hit in case of an accident?
A. That is exactly the point. Try putting a sign in your car that says, "Moron on Board," and see what happens.

Q. When a boy is named after his dad, he is called 'Junior,' but what do you call a girl that is named after her mother?
A. She is also "Junior." The word junior is genderless. However, if a girl is called junior and she has a brother who is also a junior we have a strange family. To tell each other apart we would need to create nicknames, which is what the children should have been named in the first place.

Q. How important does a person have to be before they are considered assassinated instead of just murdered?
A. They have to be considered important to be assassinated. You don't need to worry because no one will assassinate you. You might want to hide that special $20 bill you keep in the back of your wallet that you have told everyone that you keep it for emergencies. Someone might murder you for it.

Q. If you can wave a fan, and you can wave a club, can you wave a fan club?
A. You silly play on words guy! The only thing you can do with a fan club is wave at them since they will never let you be a member.

Q. If you can't drink and drive, why do bars have parking lots?
A. That is so you will know where to get your car after you sober up in some alley three miles away.

Q. If you get into a taxi cab, and ask the driver to drive backwards to your destination, will the cab driver owe you money?
A. You have it all wrong. If he drives backwards you should owe him double. But really, that is not what a taxi driver is paid to do. He drives you to destinations, not do stunt tricks for pay.

Q. If you jog backwards, will you gain weight?
A. Only if you are eating a super-sized big mac, a large chocolate cake and a box of donuts and don't drop anything.

Q. Why is Donkey Kong called "DONKEY" Kong if he's a monkey?
A. He is not the King Kong that you think he is. Have you ever noticed that he would lose every game he is in if you didn't help him? Without help, he is as smart as a donkey.

Q. Why do we teach kids that violence is not the answer and then have them read about wars in school that solved problems?
A. Look deeper into your thought. How many people were killed, how much money was wasted? Could there have been a better answer to the problem besides going to war? Learn from history instead of criticizing history.

Q. How come you pay extra to get something put on your hamburger but they don't take off the price if you get something taken off?
A. You are right. I think you should demand a discount for holding the lettuce and removing the pickle. If they say it is included in the price, then demand they give them to you separately from the hamburger.

Q. Did Noah have woodpeckers on the ark? If he did, where did he keep them?
A. Locked in a cage until he felt it was the right time to let them go. Do you think Noah allowed all the birds and animals to just wonder around the ark?

Q. What happens if your snot freezes in your nose?
A. Well it is going to be there until you get inside and allow it to thaw. You could pick at it but that might pull off your skin. Or ask someone to pick it for you. It is always great to share.

Q. Why does Donald Duck wear a towel when he comes out of the shower, when he doesn't usually wear any pants?
A. He has a towel to dry off his feathers from the shower. He doesn't wear pants because he doesn't have a pecker, chickens do.

Q. If mars had earthquakes would they be called mars quakes?
A. Of course, the earth can't quake on Mars.

Q. Why do all superheroes wear spandex?
A. Sponsors paid for their costumes.

Q. If heat rises, then shouldn't hell be cold?
A. Where do you think the heat came from?

Q. Can a stupid person be a smart-ass?
A. Congratulations. You have asked a question about yourself and I am sure you already know the answer.

Q. Why is chopsticks one of the easiest songs to play on the piano, but the hardest thing to eat with?
A. Over a billion people in China eat with chopsticks but can't play chopsticks on the piano. Your question is not based on facts but on your own biased opinion.

Q. What happens if you put this side up face down while popping microwave popcorn?
A. All of the popcorn will pop upside down.

Q. Isn't it funny how the word 'politics' is made up of the words 'poli' meaning 'many' in Latin, and 'tics' as in 'bloodsucking creatures'?
A. Funny but true. Politics tends to turn good meaning people into the bloodsucking creatures that they ran for office to stop.

Q. Why is clear considered a color?
A. We checked our 256-color box of Crayola Crayons and could not find clear. It is either invisible or you are wrong.

Q. Have you ever noticed that if you rearranged the letters in mother in law, they come out as Woman Hitler?
A. You better behave, her oven might not just be for baking.

Q. If it is illegal to park in a handicapped parking space is it also illegal to use a handicapped toilet?
A. Yes, a $250 fine in each case. Might be worth paying the fine when you have that diarrhea urge at Wal-Mart.

Q. Why did Yankee Doodle name the feather in his hat Macaroni?
A. Macaroni was the name of his horse.

Q. What is the speed of dark?
A. Zero. Dark does not move, only light moves and it moves into dark.

Q. When dog food is new and improved tasting, who tests it?
A. You can volunteer your dog Fido to test dog food, but the best way for you to be sure it is new and improved is to sample it yourself. We suggest that you purchase multiple brands and then you and Fido blind sample them together. Could be fun.

Q. If athletes get athlete's foot, do astronauts get mistletoe?
A. Very funny. If we say yes, that will account for you having small cox.

Q. If everything is part of a whole, what is the whole part of?
A. It is part of the sum.

Q. What if you were to ask a genie to grant you more than three wishes for one of you wishes?
A. You are a genius. For your first wish ask for unlimited wishes. For your second wish ask for your enemy to get double of anything you wish for. Then wish for 20 beautiful women to fall in love with you. For your next wish, wish for your sex drive to be cut in half. That should be enough for the first day.

Q. Are you telling the truth if you lie in bed?
A. Of course not, you couldn't tell the truth if you were standing in bed.

Q. Are you breaking the law if you drive past those road signs that say "Do Not Pass"?
A. You are confusing the word passed with past. The road sign has nothing to do with the past except if you passed someone after the sign.

Q. Is a lightning rod on top of church a lack of faith?
A. No, it does 2 things. First it keeps the building insurance rate down. Second, it protects the church if God gets angry at anyone sinning in the congregation.

Q. How come only your fingers and toes get wrinkly in water and nothing else does?
A. I think you should look a little closer. See if there are any wrinkles inside of your swim trunks.

Q. A pack of gum says 10 calories per piece, is that amount for chewing it or for swallowing it?
A. That is a swallow answer. You can have an entire chocolate cake at zero calories if you chew it, don't swallow and spit it out.

Q. How many questions in this book did you get right?
A. If you got more than 50% of the answers correctly you are a possible candidate to be a true wise guy.

ABOUT THE AUTHOR

Bruce R. Kindig is a retired teacher from the Davenport Community School district where he taught various history classes. He also taught American History as an adjunct professor at Scott Community College. He has a B.A. and M.A. degree in history from the University of Northern Iowa and 46 years of teaching experience. As an accomplished author, with several book review awards, he stays active with writing projects. All of his books can be found on Amazon.com.

His latest book is**: The Evil Party.** This is a primer of the origins of the United States Declaration of Independence, Constitution and the Bill of Rights. Drawing from Judeo-Christian traditions, ancient Greece and the Roman Republic and the founding of this country we see a struggle between good and evil. Those who practice evil do it for their own growth of wealth and power at the expense of various minority groups. The Democratic Party is seen as the evil party both in the reason for its founding and in the practices it used in the past and still uses today. This is explored in its history of favoring slavery, segregation and white supremacy. The policies of Presidents Jackson, Van Buren, Wilson, F. Roosevelt, Lyndon Johnson, Clinton and Obama are harmful to minorities and now critical race theory, political correctness and white privilege is used to push a socialist agenda. This book is about the evil the Democratic Party has pushed for its own wealth and power.

OTHER BOOKS WRITTEN BY BRUCE R. KINDIG

His first book was a Civil War regimental history called ***Courage and Devotion: A History of Bankhead's/Scott's Tennessee Battery***. This book has received several book review awards and is known for its focus on detail.

He has written his own autobiography entitled: ***A Good Time to Live***. Here he focuses on the last half of the 20th century from a socio-economic perspective with details on his genealogy and family.

Focusing on a teenage audience his book, ***George Washington Starts a War***, is a primer on the French and Indian War with a focus on George Washington who has the distinction of starting a war in his youth and ending a war in his maturity.

The Origins of Military Theory in World War I is a scholarly look at a subject every history student has studied. The focus is not the typical diplomatic approach but instead an evaluation of military theorists from Clausewitz to Foch.

Peace Proposals of the First World War, is about the little know diplomatic attempts at peace from 1914 through the Treaty of Brest-Litovsk. It discusses why peace could not be negotiated and why; in spite of the seriousness of those who wanted a just peace.

Essays in Military Leaders is a collection of three essays. The first essay is about Hannibal and Scipio Africanus and the development of Roman tactics in the Second Punic War. With Julius Caesar, we develop his philosophy of war by examining the strategy and tactics of the Gallic Wars. Finally, we examine the philosophy of history from the author of *On War*, Carl von Clausewitz. The descriptions are all in their own words.

Finally, Bruce R. Kindig has written a non-historical work. Combining good advice with humor he writes under the pen name John H. Marsh, ***Words of Wisdom from Anonymous Wise Guys***. Through a question format he answers the dumb questions people often ask like "what are two things you should never ask in bed"? It is the prequel to this book.

www.ingramcontent.com/pod-product-compliance
Lightning Source LLC
LaVergne TN
LVHW041607070526
838199LV00052B/3026